WHITE INDIANS

Being the First Part of Two

MICHAEL GILLS

WITH AN INTRODUCTION BY PAUL CRENSHAW

GUIDE DOG
BOOKS

White Indians © 2013 by Michael Gills

ISBN 978-1-935738-31-2

Library of Congress Control Number: 2013949322

First Edition, Fall 2013

Cover Design by Shaun Ledgerwood

www.ShaunLedgerwood.com.com

Layout by D. Harlan Wilson

www.DHarlanWilson.com

Guide Dog Books

Bowie, MD

www.GuideDogBooks.com

ACKNOWLEDGMENT

The author wishes to thank Jennifer Barnes, D. Harlan Wilson, Sean Leonard and all the good folks at Raw Dog Screaming Press. Appreciation goes out to one-time students, readers and writers par excellence Paul Crenshaw and Alycia Parnell. Thanks to Diane Wakoski and, as ever, enduring gratitude to the maestro, Fred Chappell. Grateful acknowledgment is given to the editors of the following publications where various forms of these works originally appeared:

"What the Newly Dead Don't Know but Learn," *Night Train* (ed. Rusty Barnes) and, in another form, *Industrial Workers of the World Book Review* (ed. William Hastings).

"Earth's Last Night," *Wasatch Journal* (ed. Dorothee Kocks).

Part 11 of *White Indians*, *Salt Flats Annual* (ed. Danna Sides).

CONTENTS

Metakuye Oyasin—for all my relations.

Introduction

Last Christmas I drove with my wife and daughters from North Carolina to Arkansas. Past Memphis, headed west, the land flattens out into rice fields. In winter, the fields lie fallow, rows furrowed with water. Rusted hulks of spraying equipment, old pumps, and abandoned tractors stand solitary against the winter sky. Here and there a small house sits along a raised dirt road, a one-room church rises from the sodden ground, a liquor store blinks neon in a gravel wash.

As I drive, I think of this land as prose—occasionally some idea, like rusted farm machinery or the long lines between the rows of crops—popping into my head, some image drawn from landscape and journey, from crossing through land we know by heart to someplace with which we are not familiar. It's no coincidence some of the essays in this collection are set here. Near Little Rock, I see the signs for Lonoke County, where Michael Gills is from. My destination is farther west, but I feel the same threads here. Going home. Trying to find home. Landscape as eye of the world. Family and remembrance. A search for meaning.

Driving, I think of "White Indians," where the journey and what we learn on the journey become one and the same, and "Earth's Last Night," and how fear can form inside us like a speck of dust, to, perhaps, form a pearl of wisdom and understanding. When I see the signs for Camp Robinson I think of the essay "What the Newly Dead Don't Know but Learn." To the south lies the Saline River where the dead crossed over. I can't see the river, but the essay is in my head—the cold water, the great tragedy, what carries on in the aftermath of such a thing, the making sense of it, if sense can be made.

In a few hours we will spill out of the car and into the ceremony of family—trees, presents, time spent with those we love, and I will think of the Sundance, which is often called, simply, ceremony. Ritual. The thing itself is sacred, much like the act surrounding it. Tending a fire, building a gate, shoring up a rickety platform for a water container, crossing a river, driving through fire—all are acts of ceremony.

The Sundance ceremony teaches us that everything is holy: fire, water, wind, earth, spirit. In "What the Newly Dead Don't Know but Learn" we cross rivers. In "Earth's Last Night" fire comes over the mountains. And in "White Indians" the wind howls out of the desert and the spirit moves among the gathered, those seeking what it means to be human, to stand on this good earth and be forgiving, ask forgiveness.

Gills asks us, just as he asks himself, what we consider holy, what we value above all other things, what visions we might have standing on the mountainside under the spinning stars. Work is holy, for it is through work that we seek to better ourselves. Water is holy, from the Saline River to the parched mountains of Utah and New Mexico, to the lake shining blue beneath the fire that might end the earth. The parched dancers dream of water, and in the desert heat a cold rain becomes a thing of beauty, a drop of water on the tongue a reason to contemplate the purity of the earth.

And writing is holy, an attempt to make sense of the world, whether the tragic world we survived as children or the changing world we try to survive as adults, the hurt and longing that invade us at times, the pure hard miracle of the sun on mountains on a morning in mid-July when we leave our families behind and drive south, or west, searching for something we can't define. Writing is building, much like the gates of ceremony, painstakingly crafted out of raw parts. A tree is raised, another burned. Hooks tear at the flesh, then crack like whips, and we get the sense reading these essays that more than flesh has been ripped, more than tethers torn away. Like the piece itself, the ceremony becomes an act of invention, a chance to find oneself, to assess and repair the lines and sentences that make up who we are as human beings.

Reading these works, I begin to see everything as journey. Return. What we have found along the way, what rocks and remembrances we carry with us until we find the matching piece. Soon we will climb in the car and make the long drive back to North Carolina. I will see the rusted farm machinery, the tin-roofed liquor stores, the one-room churches. I will cross rivers and mountains through snow and rain, and all that I have seen and experienced will be carried along with me, much the way, on his return from Sundance, Gills camps for the night alongside a river and watches the sun go down, the moon rise, the river rushing below him, the stars springing up above, the earth spinning in the heavens, the world on its course, the journey almost completed, the family waiting at the end.

What we find—the author, you, me—may differ. Should differ. But near the end, we realize we are all looking for the same thing.

At ceremony, Gills tells us of a man named True Heart's prayer, saying, "His prayer is all about the four directions from whence we've come, about how the ones we've left behind and who've gone away from us are here now, in our hearts. His voice speaks to me of the rootedness we seek, called so many names by so many tongues."

The ones we've left behind, but carry with us. The ones we have never left.

This is the year, driving toward my people, the ones I left behind when I moved ten years ago, this is the year the world is supposed to end. December twenty-first we are on the road, through the mountains of North Carolina and the vast long stretch of Tennessee. We joke about the Mayan calendar, how the belief that the world will end has been manufactured by latter-day prophets, shills trying to fleece the ignorant. But still, as we cross the Appalachians in a snow driven sideways by the fierce wind in the pre-morning dark, then cross the continental divide and start down the other side while the sun rises in our eyes like a great ball of fire—still, there's a moment where I wonder. Christmas night a house burns in my hometown, and as we drive back to North Carolina a few days later the ruins are still smoldering. In "Earth's Last Night" a great fire rages, and if it were the last night of the earth, what would we do?

There's another scene at the end of this great book, this attempt to find meaning in the things we call our lives, but I will leave it to be found. Only to say that there is fire. A simple fire, not the end of the end, but for Michael Gills something ends and something begins.

Driving home on the last day of the Mayan calendar, I wonder about the end, and what words should be written, what words should be said. How do we want the world to remember us? What will be our last prayer, our last thought?

The words contained in this book would be a good place to start.

Paul Crenshaw
North Carolina, March 2013

Paul Crenshaw's stories and essays have appeared or are forthcoming in Best American Essays 2005 *and* 2011, *anthologies by W.W. Norton and Houghton Mifflin, and numerous literary journals, including* Ecotone, Glimmer Train, North American Review, *and* Southern Humanities Review. *He teaches writing and literature at Elon University.*

What the Newly Dead Don't Know but Learn

My cousin found a hand-grenade in a Camp Robinson stock pond that summer, pulled the pin and tossed it at me. *Die,* he said, then took off horseback in a cloud of Arkansas dust. The thing thudded at my feet where I froze, just shut my eyes and waited. That's how it was that summer, dry, no rain since springtime when Grandfather's magnolias had bloomed like big white hands and Mama and Daddy had started burning each others' clothes in the backyard trash drum. I got sent to live with Uncle Earl, her crazy brother who ran Diamond V Stables, weekend trail rides for a $100 a pop on Camp Robinson, this vast commune where the Guard trained and it was not uncommon to find a booby-trap behind every bush. Somebody'd brought a dog that carried a live box turtle around in its mouth—the head and legs appearing then disappearing, here-gone, here-gone, the dog didn't seem to care two shits either way.

Mama'd thought it a good idea for me to help Uncle Earl with his trail ride business, though what I mostly did was ride in the back of the pickup with Butchy, his derelict son, up to the car lot—Uncle Earl's *other* business—to pump up tires on all the jalopies that had gone flat overnight. For lunch we'd sit in the air-conditioned office where it was cold enough to hang meat, eat cheeseburgers from the stand across the street, and Earl would make a run out Asher for broken down cars to sell to poor people.

WE TOTE THE NOTE, his sign said. This one afternoon, three teen-agers walked into the car lot office and tried to rob us, only Butch pulled Maggie out of its hideout holster under the desk, waved the .357 magnum in their faces, so they ran out the door into the heat screaming and we didn't see them again. The trail ride business—I don't know how all that started, but that's what everybody in Saline County with a hundred bucks wanted to do that summer, pack saddle bags with hot whiskey and ride. Maybe it was the weather that made everybody crazy. Twenty-some had signed on, their horse trailers all parked in the base parking lot, tents spread across a field where wild daisies bloomed right up to the algae-covered pond where Butchy'd sliced open his heel on a broken bottle before finding the grenade.

I'd seen Maxie sneak into Earl's white teepee, followed by the spotted dog with the turtle wriggling in its mouth. Macky Smith—this friend of Earl's who was training to be an Oaklawn jockey though he was way too big—saw it too, and we both heard. Macky was currying the mane and tail of the Palomino he'd broken that summer, a spirited horse who neighed at the other horses with nostrils flared, whose eyes were curious and human-like—you could see the horse figure out what was coming next—it was amazing. *May Day,* he was called.

Somebody'd said the dog thought he *owned* the turtle, that it was his possession, I remember willing it to live and out came its head. If you got close enough to see, some family or another had painted their names on the bottom of the shell, only it was from twelve years ago when I wasn't even born yet, the oddness of that.

My Welsh pony was trained to lie down and hold his breath, a good trick because I could ride out ahead of everyone else and say, "Blaze, lay down and hold your breath." Up Maxie rode on her big paint. "*Oh!*" she cried out, the same word that she screamed inside Earl's white teepee. "*Oh!*" she said. "*He's bloating.*"

The paint stamped its feet, snorted. "Be still, goddamnit," she said, hooked a heel in the stirrup, swivelled off and wrapped both perfumed arms around me, so that I could smell her dark hair, like magnolias in a bowl at the center of the dinner table while Mama prayed a too long prayer. "I'm sorry, son," she said.

I waited, breathing her in, that much I'd learned.

"Get up, Blaze," I said, and the horse straightened its front legs, hopped up and shook the dirt off, trotted to me, nuzzling my arm with a nicker.

"*You*," Maxie said. She frowned. "Ever heard of the boy who cried wolf?"

I had no idea where the main trail ride was going, but I'd learned to let things roll out the way they rolled out. The hand-grenade lay at my feet. I was afraid to move. The sky was blue above my head. There was a lot to think about. I mean, should you pick up a hand-grenade and throw it back? Run like hell? Go pull Maxie off Uncle and tell? Do nothing? As I ever had, I chose the latter and it brought us bad luck that very day.

Uncle had decided we'd swim the river that afternoon, cross the particular bend he'd chosen the week before when he'd driven out and camped overnight, probably with Maxie and her big paint. Horse people were funny—what class you were from kind of disappeared—shoveling shit was shoveling shit. This was Arkansas in July, and let me say two things about that. One: July is maybe not hot as August, but ungodly hot all the same—even the witchdoctors riding each other's backs seemed dazed, drunk with heat and there was zilch for breeze—the only relief, water. Two: when you're twelve, you haven't thought of some things yet, like the fine line between the truth and a lie, and that gap in-between that breathes in and out with a mystery all its own. You've sensed it, maybe even believe you can control it, but you haven't thought it out and understood the repercussions. What I'm saying is that, if you tell a lie, like your horse has lain down and died up the trail, then, when they ride up on it, yell at the thing to get up and it does. You see them shake their heads in disbelief, and it's possible that you could start to believe that you actually did have miraculous powers. I mean, you could start to believe your own bullshit about raising the dead. Well, it's possible, at least it was for me that summer. Who could blame me—my people were really fucked up—I had it in my blood by osmosis.

So Uncle Earl decided to swim horses across the Saline River on Camp Joseph T. Robinson Military, just like he'd seen in John Wayne westerns where a bunch of cowboys swam equines and cattle across some western river, which I've since learned is a crock. Despite the heat and drought, the trees were green that day, and the riparian shade was pleasing. Earl led us right up riverside on Chico—a thick-necked stud that was unstoppable once he took off, so Uncle'd replaced the chin strap with a strand of barbed-wire that bloodied the white whiskers. Butchy followed his daddy on Sugarfoot, right up to the water's edge, where Uncle climbed down out of the saddle, picked up a stick and sat cross-legged in the dirt.

"Swimming a horse is not complicated," he said, and drew a sweeping S into the dirt with the stick, marking the appointed spot in the river bend, where a low-slung tree had some moss hanging off. "Set your ferry angle against the current, lay out on his back and hang on to the saddle horn. Macky will follow me, then Maxie."

Maxie's paint nickered and May Day snorted—the stock knew something was up.

"We'll take out here," he said, marking an X lower in the bend. "Any questions?"

A cowboy wearing new shiny boots with gleaming spurs and a felt Stetson sipped from an army canteen and I saw Butch off to the side, poking a stick into a crawdad hole on the bank.

"What about life jackets?" the cowboy asked. "Don't we need life jackets?"

Uncle looked at me for some reason. He had a soft spot in his heart, because Mama was his only sister, and they'd been through the ringer growing up, and now it was happening all over again to me. "Naw," Earl said. "Just hang on to your hoss. Okay?"

He swigged at his canteen, the fake cowboy.

The water was brown, chestnut color, the hue of Blaze's mane and tail, that's what I remember, that and how personal floatation devices seemed like great, good sense. This all happened in the days before release forms and such, so a good lawyer would lick his lips at a moment like this—people who'd paid money for a trailride getting swum across an unfamiliar river on a military commune by a man who'd never thought to purchase insurance against accidental drownings or water poisoning or whatever such negligence could be ferreted out of such a situation. Maxie wore a yellow bikini top, one of the straps falling off her shoulder. I'd seen a cottonmouth riding the current downstream. It wasn't swift or anything like that, just a wrist-thick snake slipping down the current mid-river, just before all the grownups in our party rode over the marked S, passing from dirt into water, so the air was strong with fly dope and saddle leather, and the snakey smell of the mindless river itself, coiling through that summer afternoon that severed me from my childhood.

Earl swam first, big white Chico lunging into the cool eddy, so you could see his forestocks glow, even through the murk, read the bloody mist beneath the open mouth. Then Macky on May Day, Maxie on the paint, and a couple other adults in new cowboy hats and boots, the fear and thrill of what they did, how one feels, I'd later learn, when entering white water that has taken a life, the water has personality, you can feel it. Butch rode Sugarfoot, a small horse, but stocky and real spirited, a strong swimmer. Blaze would do anything I asked, so we followed last—I was sweeper. A crow caw-cawed over then, so its shadow fell across our path, and that's when it happened, mid-river, Uncle Earl screaming for us to turn back now, turn around and swim back. *Turn the fuck around*, he hollered. *Don't follow.* I'd just lain full out on Blaze's back, both his front hooves pawing water, thinking how uncannily cool this was, how easy and sweet to swim horseback. And neck reining a horse around in full swim is easier demanded than done, I've never seen it happen in any John Wayne Western, not once. But Blaze obeyed and we climbed up the undercut bank, onto a table-rock that offered a full-view of the scene that still plays out before me on nights when the house gets quiet and I can hear my wife and daughter breathing.

My people are crazy. *Good-crazy*, Mama'd say, though I've never understood what evolutionary advantage there is to having such a predicament in your bloodline. Mama's daddy cut his own leg off with a bucksaw while on a firewood expedition up on Danville Mountain, then hemorrhaged all the way to St. Mary's where an emergency surgery saved him, but only by the skin of his teeth. At seventeen, she eloped with an Air Force man who claimed his father was a legislator in Arizona, only it turned out they lived in a screenless trailer next to a Tucson plasma center. His brother was a dwarf, which means my own children could be dwarves—my children's children. After I was born, she left him, but he followed her back to Arkansas and tried to kidnap me outright, only my grandmother somehow got him thrown into Tucker Prison Farm where he picked peas for one whole summer. Then Mama married O.W., who'd been drafted as an outfielder for the New York Yankees, a flattop he-man that nobody fucked with, not even Uncle Earl, who was maybe craziest of all. Once, during spring run-off, Earl'd strapped one of those cheap-shit orange life jackets onto me and Butchy, thrown us into Mulberry River—Arkansas's premier white water— for the sixteen mile float through overhangs and strainers, amongst the most awful flotsam imaginable. We crawled out at the river bridge outside Opelo, half-drowned, caught a ride in whatever jalopy he'd had driven out for the occasion, drove back and did it again—three times in all over the course of the weekend flood.

Other times he'd have us jump off high things, cliffs and trees, a roof or two, and once he'd tied a Labrador Retriever to Butchy's foot, then swung them off a tree swing into Hurricane Creek. He wasn't right in the head, Uncle wasn't, but he owned a business, which made him respectable in Mama's eyes, enough so to keep me while her and O.W. went at each other. So it's no surprise what was about to happen, Macky Smith screaming *May Day, May Day*, the big Palomino neck-hooked on a fisherman's trotline, run straight down the middle of the S-bend in the river

Witchdoctors rode each other over the flat rock to the bank where a king snake had shed blue skin. The rest of the trail riders were off their horses on the shore, some crying out and some just staring, the way you look at a house on fire. Butch had unslung his lariat, stood knee-deep in the current with it dangling. Out there were Uncle and Macky, both swimming circles with Chico now, whose bloody chin shone in the watery glare. May Day's eyes, even from where I sat, flashed in their sockets and the neighing began, a pleading sound cadenced to the rhythmic slosh of hooves. The horse pawed water in a frenzy of muscle so the whole trotline was visible, silver hooks gleaming at measured intervals to unseen tie-offs on the far banks. I'd set this sort of line myself, those summers down on Lake Ouachita, when I'd go out with my mother's one-legged father with a roll of hundred-weight nylon line and a sackful of treble hooks. Rocking in his flat bottom, we'd tie one end to the trunk of an overhanging Cyprus, stretch line across the entirety of a deep water cove, then tie three-foot lengths of cord every six feet or so, and from these loop-knot fresh-sharpened hooks. We'd fish bream beds all afternoon until we'd scored a bucketful of bluegill, shoulder hook each and sink the whole thing with forty pound rocks on either end. After midnight, we'd run the lines in the dark, careful, because he'd known a man who'd drowned this way. "Hello? Are you listening?" the old man would say, then guide my hand to the quivering line, where it felt like we'd hooked a Volkswagen somewhere out there underneath us, and hand-line us toward what swirled in the dark. That was the kind of line May Day had swum into that afternoon in July when I was twelve and believed that I possessed special powers.

Maybe five minutes passed and I don't think anyone knew what to do—it's like that, watching a drowning. People scream for you to help them, they beg and plead and cuss and pray, but finally there's not a whole lot that can be done, and you can't turn away even. Butch was crying, the lariat swinging at his knees. His daddy was out there in the water—and it dawned on me that he loved his old man. May Day was full-fight now, *bleating*, so that the sound got inside of you and caught fire like listening to Jethro Tull's flute playing on acid. Black hooves with silver shoes made ruckus in the water, lifting the white line again and again so it showed its silver stringer of hooks for twenty feet in either direction, a nice channel cat on one down the line. Macky Smith and Uncle Earl, they clung to Chico who was fighting water too now, close enough for one of the hooks to catch any of the three. Earl was white-faced, his saddle bags spun in an eddy. I

17

could see the resemblance between him and my mother, the widow's peak and earthy eyes, the countenance with which they both faced death, and that's when I thought of my knife.

Cold water is heavier than warm, so there was a layer about four feet down that would have chilled my toes and then my foot, and then a hole where the current undercut the bank. I'd feel power in the water as my dream self slipped down, the Old Henry unfolded in my right hand. From this level, my eyes were even with the surface plane of the water and I could feel the horse screaming, a terrible sound to hear from there, a strong horse drowning. May Day'd disappear entirely, then fight his way up again, the screech constant now, the mush in his breathing, a plume of blood in the violent water. The line must be cut, I'd have to dive down, take it in my hand and saw with the other, then coax May Day to swim toward the other end, that's what I was thinking, dog-paddling, scared, my heart beating in my throat, picturing what must be done.

May Day was real, beautiful flesh and blood, tiring, about to give. Ten feet in front of me his vision shimmered, the water swished in his lungs. His eyes flashed, and we looked into each others' eyes there at the same level for a moment, long enough. I could read his mind and him mine in that second. *It's okay*, he was thinking, *here where I am now, not so bad, it's okay son. Take care of yourself.* The knife escaped my hand. And there in front of me, close enough to touch, the horse sank and the brown water stilled.

For a long time and maybe by mistake, my mother tried to contact me from the grave. It would happen in the middle of the night, me asleep beside my good and patient wife, and the phone would ring out three or four times off-kilter. When I picked up, scared shitless, no one was there, not even a breath. Then I'd crawl back in bed and hear her call my name—just like that, say my name right through the walls. It was creepy. It scared the Jesus out of me, though you must know that we were close. With me never meeting my father, she was like my sister almost. I delivered her elegy with a true joy in my heart for her life, despite the evil Baptist preachers who wanted to turn the moment into a guilt-fest and rub everybody's nose in it. But then I'd hear her voice in the night, over and over and over, it was no dream.

Buddhists believe the body goes on a forty-nine day journey after death—they call it *bardo*, the time before the soul reaches the other side. But the soul has to be willing. If somebody's a victim of foul play, for instance, well that soul might not be cool with going on *bardo*, they might be pissed off and have some talking to do. I don't know about all that, but I know for certain, without a glimmer of doubt, that Mama tried to talk to me from the grave, and it got so that I couldn't stand it, even though I missed her with my whole heart. Finally, in a way that unsettled my wife until her own mother died and she did the same, I yelled out in the dark. *Leave me alone*, I screamed. *Leave me the hell alone and die.* Around that time, her voice went away, and she has not spoken to me now for a long, long time.

Blaze nuzzled my back. I heard the soft nicker, turned, grabbed a hank of mane and let him bring me to the shore where Macky lay on his face weeping, inconsolable for an hour or more there until the shade came on and the cicadas kicked in and he finally climbed up behind Uncle on Chico and was ridden back to camp. May Day, the golden Palomino with knowing eyes, had been his solace—he loved the horse, and had finally had to retreat and let it drown. One of the fake cowboys had prayed out loud, then produced a pistol that looked like a toy compared to Maggie. Macky threw it in the river, where it lies loaded, probably, to this day. Back at camp, as dark came on and all those lightning bugs stung the bitterweed, he sat shaking his head. He set on a five-gallon bucket and shook his head.

It had fallen to me and Butch to unsaddle all the horses, feed and water and stow gear while an officer from Camp Robinson questioned Uncle Earl and some of the other adults. We loaded the horses into trailers, and it was dark when we rolled out. By the time we made it back to Diamond V, it was after midnight. I was conked out on the truck seat beside Butch when Uncle backed the trailer to the front gate, loosed the horses in a side pasture. Blaze stood out there, staring at me in the rearview. He'd suffered himself to play dead at my bidding, then leapt to life at my command. Could a horse fathom irony? Could I?

I allowed myself the vision of the three of us—me, Mama and O.W.—gone to see a movie on a February night. It was *Jungle Book*, and they held hands as big talking apes danced across the super-wide screen. We walked out and were hit in the face with an unpredicted snow, flakes big as silver dollars, our Pontiac covered already. "Ho, ho," O.W. sang out, skidding on his bootheels. Face to the sky, Mama seemed stunned. "Pixie dust," she said, and threw big wonderful handfuls up into the frosty air that was cleansed, that night, of the stench from the paper mill further south.

Earl left us in the truck cab, walked into the house and a light came on in the kitchen. I'd once seen him shoot a dog with a bow and arrow right out the front door. It was a neighbor's dog, a barker, and he'd just pulled back and shot the thing, just like that. I imagined him inside at the kitchen table, thinking how he'd marked our passage into the dirt, how he would always be the man who'd scribed the perfect entry into the S-bend.

I was twelve that year and the world looks a whole lot different from this side. I have a child now, a girl who's twelve, big beautiful eyes like her mother and her mother's mother. She plays piano, and sometimes when I cook late in the afternoon, I weigh the notes falling and rising and falling like this shimmering waterfall. The horse and I had looked each other in the eye right there at the end. I'd swum out from the dream of guilt and sorrow, with an unfolded knife and fear in my heart. I'd been too late, sure, but I can live with that. Those afternoons while I mash garlic into the skillet, throw tomatoes and parsley into the sizzle, I listen to my daughter play the notes and wish Mama could hear this song, that she would wake up and forgive me and speak to me and not be dead.

She drove us to the family cemetery once, a road that paralleled the Trail of Tears, Choctaw land that the Cherokee had once been forced to walk, out past Lanty, Arkansas into the family bottoms where every barbed wire fence was blown over with honeysuckle and blackberry. There, on a hillside that overlooked a lightning struck tree, our people were laid to rest at the feet of their fathers for the generations since they'd walked down from Henry County, Tennessee. We found their stones high on the hill, and I remember how the black-eyed Susan swayed and bloomed that morning. A hard rain had fallen and someone'd turned loose dogs. Off in the hollow we could hear them bay. Mama yanked weeds from the white pea gravel that covered her daddy, then lay a fistful of fresh picked flowers beneath his name. "Looky here," she said, and stepped off to the old man's feet. "This is my spot. And you'll be there, Mike." She pointed, "right beside me."

I looked at it.

Then Mama stood on her spot, and I on mine. She reached out a hand and I took it. She swayed one way and then the other and there, with no one watching, we danced, just shook ourselves on that piece of earth, the dogs howling in pursuit now, about to tree. The sun came out and the Solgahatchia bottoms shone below us. My mother laughed, her voice high and silvery like a girl's. We fell down laughing, I don't know why.

Earth's Last Night

Upriver, a flash of purple—only lighter, lavender, the color of redbud back in Arkansas. But this was October, the cottonwoods were yellow. For a long time I kept seeing, thinking what on earth? A woman wearing a bridal veil cast silvery line, the length of her rod moving from vertical to horizontal, vertical to horizontal.

She was thigh-deep in a ripple. "Hey? Do us a favor?"

She never missed a lick, the line singing over the pale green water.

"Sure."

"We're from Virginia," she said, and I could hear it in her voice, which is a nice thing out west, to hear your native tongue from the mouth of a pretty woman. She brushed back the lavender veil so I saw blue eyes. "This is our honeymoon."

The groom handed me their camera, joined his new wife arm in arm, smiling like there was no tomorrow.

"I'm no good at this," I said.

She smiled through gorgeous white teeth. "Just point and shoot."

"Cheese," they said, stripping off sunglasses, sunshine in their eyes.

A wild country, this.

The next summer, after my mother died out of the blue, we ran off to Flaming Gorge. The place was going to be our medicine but our arrival coincided with the first whiff of smoke. Surrounded by a million acres of national forest, white boats rocked on still water, trolling up Mackinaw. Sun shone between the ribs of the steel bridge. Jill gazed up at Mustang Ridge, just above us.

"We should check that," she said.

Just a puff, a smidgen, that's all I could see. Three weeks after laying my mother in the ground, I was thinking *uh-uh*, no way.

"Clouds. It's just a cloud."

She sipped her drink with eyes shut. "It's fire. I know it is."

This was fire country. Monuments to dead hotshots are built at every turn in the road in the Ashley National Forest.

"Fine. I'll go."

Jill brushed the side of my face with her lips. She said, "Sorry," and "hurry back."

Just like that, the moment when sparks fly.

I huffed up the cliff trail and shouldered our shovel for who knows why. Then I hiked off through the snarl of paths toward the host's RV where already three cop cars blocked the road, lights aswirl.

"*Evacuate*," a cop in dark glasses said. "Pack your stuff and leave."

I said, "What?"

The host looked confused. A second policeman was walking him through the registry notebook, calling names and license numbers. The host's wife was holding a little dog with a pink bow between its ears. Not an hour had passed since I wrote them a check for our site.

"Get out. *Leave*," the cop said.

I couldn't see his eyes, but the voice held an edge, like I'd started the fire. "Now?"

He stared me through. And when I looked back he was still staring, burning holes in my back, a thin grey plume rising behind him. The day was hot and clear—perfect lake weather. And the water was cold. The thought of repacking, humping gear in the godawful heat, didn't seem fair. We were being cheated. I'd paid money down for our site. We were grieving. Forget you, I said out loud.

On the horizon danced the first tongues of flame, a sight that froze me. Tangled in smoke, the mute blaze rose up. I could feel it on my face, under my teeth. A helicopter'd taken to the sky. We saw it over the lake, whipping the water into little whitecaps. Lyra colored in the Bugs Bunny book we'd bought for her in Arkansas. All during the funeral, while the Baptist preachers gave their best shot at making us feel like scum, my daughter colored a rabbit. "Is MaMa hungry in her casket?" she'd asked.

I was loading the kitchen into an ammo box when the pair of cops slammed up.

"This is it," the one with glasses said. He gripped his pistol butt, I swear to god. He put his hand on his gun, "Leave those dogs." He leaped into the car and screamed off with sirens full-blare. Beyond, the fire was catching its breath, you could hear tree bark pop and burn. Leave our dogs—what kind of person does that.

From then on it was katy-bar-the-door. Jill and Lyra crammed into the front seat with one lab at their feet. I shoved Venus in back with the remainder of our ramshackle gear. The thing was, we stayed cool, we didn't miss a beat. Not even Lyra. Above, someone directed us over a loud speaker, the blades whipping dirt and pine needles. We weren't even breathing hard, here in the valley of the shadow of death. Our heart rates, I'm convinced, were not elevated. I turned the key and the engine caught, pushed in the clutch and downshifted to first. The helicopter barked unintelligible words above us. Up the one road out, fire was about to cross, a red tsunami. I drove straight into it, this quiet place, thinking this is it, here she is.

The road out was two narrow lanes, fairly straight, though there was one stretch with a hard S-turn, a steep switchback. We were the very last. The helicopter flew straight above us. Our windows were down. Roaring to our left, the fire was near enough to have sucked the oxygen, and therefore sound, from the air. I would later learn that we drove into an actual vacuum. They'd name it Mustang, after the ridge where it ignited. We entered the fire's inner-sanctum—pure silence. On our faces was writ the memory of ages, what has ever destroyed and preserved our kind. Here was death everlasting, and here was the path to life. I didn't think all that, but I felt it, and I knew that I was not the first nor the last to think such thoughts. The fire cathected me, it wired me in and I felt deeply human and loved myself and my wife and my daughter in our dying moments. I remembered, as if from another life, that I'd strapped our propane tank, the one from the grill at home, on top of the Pathfinder. And in that way we drove into the flame.

My hands turned white. There was a single moment when I was sure that it was over and I felt Jill's hand on mine, how she reached back at the same time and touched Lyra's face. I pushed the button that rolled the windows up tight and that thin glass alone was between us and it. The drive itself was maybe five miles. Cop cars flashed a quarter-mile out on the main road, Highway 191, that ran down into Dutch John and River Road.

I've heard that it's possible to see things through peripheral vision that elude full sight. The fire was neither young nor old. The fire made much seem ridiculous. The language the fire made was *now*. The word the fire said was *yes*. I loved the fire. I feared it as no other. My wife and daughter were far away now. The fire was the quickening before birth.

I drove past the cops, past Dutch John's gas station with the sea-green Volvo up on stilts, onto the highway to a rest area that overlooked the gorge. When we stopped, I looked for a second at the tremendous burning, a cloud that resembled still photos of mushroom clouds, nuclear bombs, fission. A ski boat towed a slalom skier who took a mighty leap across the wake, sliced the glass-still water. The fire was behind him. He did not seem bothered. That was us, where we'd come from, who we were now.

Flaming Gorge Lodge was sleepy, they'd all seen this sort of thing before, the wait staff and guides, no big deal. A world record Mackinaw trout with a pouch of Skittles in its mouth hung on the wall behind the hotel clerk's counter. We were shaky. Behind us, in our wake, the town of Dutch John was being evacuated, the fire on it like a hurricane.

"Can I help you," the woman behind the counter said.

I said, "I hope so," and asked for a room, whatever she had. "We have dogs," I said for some reason. "They're good dogs. We've been in the fire."

She raised her brows. "Fire?"

I pointed out the plate glass window. "Mustang Ridge," I said. "It's on fire. We're the last folks out." Hearing myself say it made it real. Out in the truck, Jill and Lyra were blank-eyed stargazers, light in their eyes.

"Oh," she said. "Oh." She smiled as if the fire was her one-eyed cousin, popping the glass-eye out of its socket for laughs. "We have double queens, no smoking. The special tonight is prime rib. Will that be a credit card?"

A few more vehicles pulled into the parking lot, and those families no doubt found rooms just like us, for the place still dozed at three o'clock on a summer day in June with the earth on fire. Nobody had an inkling of what was coming, what we were up against, even us who'd looked it in the face.

I handed Jill the keys, started the truck and drove up to the motel-style rooms, backed into our slot outside the front door and porch, where sat white plastic chairs and an ice bucket.

People were getting here now; outside the main office there was no parking. We'd been just right on the inside cusp. Dutch John, the town settled by people who'd built Flaming Gorge Dam back in the '60s, was being evacuated. I recognized Emmett Heath, *Fly Rod & Reel's* Guide of the Year in '92. A man who looked like his brother was with him—the two big as bears, wearing flip-flops and cut-offs. Inside the cool room, Jill was on the phone with her father long distance to Florida, trying to explain. Two men from Wisconsin unlocked the room that shared our porch. Lyra had started the room's pre-loaded video—a film about fly-fishing the scenic Green, reading the hatch, tying the blood-knot.

Jill was telling her father about passing through the fire. She didn't want to scare him, that was not her intent at all. But she needed for him to *know*.

She needed for him to register that road on fire.

"Dad," she said, finally, "It was like watching the world end, Earth's last night."

On the television screen, a woman in a broad-brimmed hat had just landed a healthy rainbow. It lay doubled in a net held by an invisible hand, shining, fighting to spit out the hook. Like a freight train barreling down my heart, it dawned on me that I couldn't call my mother. Not in a million years, I'd never hear her voice again.

"No. We're okay. We're fine," Jill told her father. "I promise."

The fire had burned the power lines from the dam's hydroelectric plant, so we ate our supper in the dark lodge restaurant where the generators hummed in the foyer and every last table was telling its own version of the Mustang story, the one that would become famous for years and years in these parts of Wyoming, Colorado and Utah.

"A thing happened out there I'll never forget."

"I'm forgetting already," another said, off to our left.

"She's all on fire now. Just look."

Through the plate glass windows over which hung stuffed moose, cougar and elk with Christmas tinsel glittering in the kerosene light, the glow was something you keep seeing with eyes shut. The fire surprised. It shone from some chasm that had opened up between the earth's crust and core.

Four-year-old Lyra, "Daddy? You said we could swim-swim."

"Eat your corn," Jill said. She sloshed more red wine into a coffee mug and filled mine to boot.

"Daddy said swim-swim."

"No. I love you," she said, and that was that.

Firefighters were arriving by the truckload now, setting up a tent city on the four-acre lot where guides stored covered dories. I've seen them before, the hotshots, flown in from the Apache Reservations in Arizona, a whole platoon from Rome, Georgia—they come from all over, lugging fire suits and axes and breathing masks and air tanks. The parking lot was filled with campers, RVs and state troopers. Some National Guard troops were beginning to stand in. Dutch John was empty, the fire about to plow over the millionaires' helicopter pads and on to the Green River which it leapt in one slick move. An emergency kitchen was constructed outside the Flaming Bait, Tackle and Liquor, ramshackle camp tables set up with Coleman stoves and propane lanterns.

Lyra ate her corn.

Jill said, "We're supposed to get something out of this. It's some kind of sign."

A half-pound hunk of prime rib arrived with hot salted fries and a glass of ice tea, what seemed to me like the best meal ever to appear in this lifetime. There was ketchup on the table, A1 and Heinz 57. Sweating in our cooler back in the Pathfinder, we had steaks, fat ribeyes from grass-fed cows they charge your nuts off for at Wild Oats, but who cared? We were jangled—cooking was beyond us.

"End of June. Today's the last day of June."

"But what *day* is it."

A deep voice from one table over said, "*Fire*, man."

Silence caved in around us, and I thought of the vacuum—when it sucked the oxygen from our lungs. Jill and I knocked down our prime rib and listened while outside shimmied and glowed. The whole thing about Utah, everything looks like a movie set, these spectacular backdrops. And now the Uintas on fire.

A waitress bussed our plates and apologized for running out of coffee. "We given it all to the fire boys," she said.

I asked how to pay.

"Room?"

"118."

"You're lucky," she said. "Most of them are going without tonight. Course, I'm making room," she sighed. "I'll tack it on. Just sign this, hon."

Lyra'd fallen asleep in her booster. Her head tilted at a painful angle. I lifted her, held her to my chest, felt her heart beat into my own. Mama always said, the child becomes your life.

"Maybe we're not listening like we should," Jill said as I signed off, figured the tip. "We've got to open up." She said, "This is our *life*."

"I'm all ears," I said. "I'm wide-flipping open."

We watched the world burn, sitting in plastic chairs on the porch, Lyra asleep in her sunflower jammies on one of the double beds. The Wisconsin fishermen were too plowed for knot tying so they joined us with their own plastic chairs while people I couldn't see made one hell of a party in the gravel parking lot. These fishermen, they'd driven all the way from Wisconsin for the blue ribbon fishery here. They'd planned their vacations out a year in advance, had practiced themselves into topnotch casters. They'd watched the fly-fishing video a dozen times before the power lines burned through, and were glad for the peace and quiet, despite the party off to our left, where people were carrying on something awful, like a hurricane party back east.

Here we were, Wisconsin fishermen, a lawnful of partygoers and the biggest fire on the continent—and none of us with even the foggiest idea of how to behave in such company. We were on the mountainside, the eastern slope of the Uintas, staring into a sea of flames.

"So you people—what's *your* story?"

Jill sat just beside me. She'd run a tubful of cold water, bathed, and I could smell the sweetness on her skin. "*Story?*"

Nights are cool in the Uintas—down in the fifties now. Pine scented the air, the wind had turned the smoke away from us. It was very pleasant and the fire held our gaze.

"What landed you here?"

"Long or short?"

Down in the parking lot, hundreds stood still as stone, staring east, the makeshift soup kitchen going full-throttle, and every now and then another truckful of hotshots would show up in yellow helmets. Eleven o'clock, maybe, surely it was before midnight. Red lights glowed on the sides of RVs, their generators humming. Somebody'd found a bagful of balloons and a full fledge water balloon fight had broken out. One of the Dutch John women had stuck two real full ones inside her blouse and danced on the lawn to a car radio that played "Honky Tonk Blues." A fat balloon splatted on the porch beside me—Lyra'd like this, balloons.

"My mother died three weeks ago," I heard myself say.

"I'm sorry," one said.

"Me, too," said the other.

Vodka has a blue sheen that goes lucent as slag glass in firelight. I said, "It's okay. No, it's fine." It's a little embarrassing, I've learned, having someone die. On the other hand, it gets you attention, makes people seem to care about who you are, what you're about. "We came here for peace."

"Peace," one said.

"I know what you're saying," said the other.

These fishermen, there was something calming in their voices, like they were somehow meant to be here at the end of it all, and the fire out there burning wasn't so bad at all, more like something that you know and recognize in your heart as right and good and inevitable, though a surprise nonetheless. I hear myself break into the story I'd learn to tell for the rest of my life, the one that would become an heirloom for my people, how we drove the road through the valley of the shadow and lived to tell. I made it clear that this all happened in the wake of my mother's death, and left it at that.

The dancing woman swished our way. "We should have a fire *every* night," she said and was gone.

Above us, risen on the horizon, the fat Strawberry Moon was blood red. I hadn't seen it coming—none of it, not for a long way back. This smoke-wreathed moon was alien, a shock, related in no way to anything I'd ever seen. Later, before sleep, Jill touched my face, traced either side of my lips. Corny, something straight off a Hallmark card, but I felt her fingertips and knew that in the end, love wins all.

I woke to a glow that was outside and inside. I was thinking two things at the same time, if that's possible. The first, I don't know why, was about that Brueghel painting that shows the fall of Icarus, though the boy's death is only a backdrop against the gardener gardening and the shepherd shepherding sheep that munch the grassy hillside, a nice day with ships sailing, the wind puffing white sails—a day just like today had been.

And the other thought was of that bride in the water. I thought of her laying the line out over the hole that darkened beneath a desert varnished boulder, the sort the Anasazi chose for infinite spirals. On fire this second, the river corridor will burn clear to Colorado and a thousand firefighters will conjoin here, a unit of which is southern—Rome, Georgia—who'll see this country for the first time. They'll fall in love and dream of their mothers at night while they sleep on the ground and coyotes yowl off the eastern banks. The fire will glow on their faces and they'll dream themselves children again, inhabiting that place where the day is forever at hand. Lost loves will beckon them inside rooms where time is still and hope unfazed. Cool ash will flutter from above, turn the water black from here to Arizona, and in springtime the mountains will erupt and be furious with life.

WHITE INDIANS
Sundance. Zuni Territory, New Mexico. July 2005.

There is among the Hopi and other tribes a
prophecy of the return of Pahana—the lost white
brother—and with this arrival comes the last days
and end of the fourth world.

1.

My uncle once talked me into pissing on an electric fence—what a surprise that was. "Go ahead," he dared, "you don't have a hair." Fenceposts strung with silver wires stretched across two pastures to the barn where a big electric box had a lightning bolt zig-zagged across its face. Uncle grabbed the middle strand, squeezed. Through a lip-trembling smile he said, "What you afraid of boy?" Thirty years later, the question remains. There was a still moment in the back pasture, pieces of light flickering through the woods, when I hooked up to it. All this Indian stuff, at least for me, it's like that, pissing on an electric fence. *Whoa*, I remember thinking, *that's something*.

A week before ceremony, I come across two dead magpie, run over on the road up to the foothills where we hike Sundays—our *church,* we call it. One's deader than hell. The other, I'm not sure. July 10, the snakes are out. I'm hungover. In six days I leave for Zuni and Sundance—my conscious life is shifting gears, mutating, that's how it seems. I've dreamed of Mama, three years dead now, and the look on her face when we crossed each other's path, the shock followed by tears followed by joy. Her chin quivered. She said my name and we held each other. Just like that, in some dreamland where everybody's walking all night and all day, and there's Mama, we're reunited. A week ago, 4th of July weekend, my wife, daughter and I rescued eight yahoo rafters out of Mother-In-Law Rapid on the Green River below Flaming Gorge Dam. They came barrel-assing past a house-sized rock with life jackets unbuckled, kids, old ladies and all thrown flailing into the stiff eddy beneath. We hauled them out, all eight, though it took a while, and their shit was spread over a quarter mile of river. A hefty woman from Oklahoma got her foot caught and almost drowned. Her husband let her go but somehow managed to keep hands on a styro-cooler full of iced Milwaukee's Best, which I drank a good many of while rowing all thousand pounds plus of them down river to Little Hole where they thanked us and limped off—our first rescue. Four miles down, we camped. I hooked a brown trout and an osprey trilled overhead, throwing shadow wings on the green water. That night we drank whiskey beside a wood fire while the sun went down and coyotes kicked in.

Life's got strange on me, and these magpie, I see them from a long way off.

We coast to a stop. Beside me, Lyra sees, flinches. She was four years old when Mama died, kept asking, "Is MaMa cold in her casket?"

I open the door, pull the e-brake.

"What are you doing?" Jill asks, a fair question. "Please don't touch that thing."

Out in the street, I lift one of the dead birds and carry it to a tree. Its mate flutters. The tail feathers are a foot-long, unearthly green. I've read how ghostdancers wear Magpie colors. They dance all night praying for the world to crack open and come, for the resurrection of their ancestors, for the birth of White Buffalo Calf and the return of *Pahana*—the lost white brother. I lay the first bird under a cottonwood. The second one shrieks when I touch it, very much alive. It looks me in the eye, warm in my hand, its heart beating hard and fast. *Mitakuye Oyasin*, all my relations, what the Lakota say. When I lay him down, the beak opens and it's dark inside. I'm sorry for the thing.

These Sunday church hikes, I'll pick up a candy wrapper, say something self-righteous like "Don't shit in my temple," and Lyra will say, "Daddy?" We burn sage up in the foothills where springs leak and prayer bundles are tied into the treelimbs of Mountain Mahogany, the thin-leafed trees with silver bark that grow out of rocks on the saddles between buttes. Today, an Italian guy hikes behind us. The climb is steep and, by the time we reach the rock house we're breathing hard, sweating. Outlined above is Red Butte, a ridgeline slide where Mormon pioneers quarried hearth stones.

A rattlesnake swims across the footpath. Of a sudden, it takes the breath.

"Snake!" my daughter screams. Jill leaps backward, fear-eyed. The Italian's never seen a rattlesnake and we all stand gawking at the thing above the rock house. Its body makes sharp angles as it moves, triangulate head the color of rock dust. Its eyes shine. There's a smell; a whiff of scent hits a nerve. For a few seconds this rattler doesn't sense us, then goes electric, and that electricity infects us. Two feet off the trail the thing settles, sun in its eyes.

My wife, daughter and the Italian pass, they haul ass, let feet touch the earth as seldom as possible, and keep on going. But I sense a moment here, a chance. This is important, I'm thinking. Here's a crevice, an in-between moment. No accidents in this life. "*Ah-ho,*" I say out loud, "brother rattlesnake." And that split-second, just as sound leaves my lips, the snake unhinges its jaws and fully extends both fangs. A thin venom stream sprays from each. It lay there, the snow-white fangs narrowing to pinpoints, the forked tongue tasting me. Snake medicine is initiation, initiation is death. These serpents dance upright in dark dens, I've read, they sway and counter-sway for many dark days. I back away—the image tattooed on my mind's eye.

How I got myself into all this—the Indian stuff—beats the shit out of me. I rode my horse over ice once when I was a kid. In Arkansas, a hard freeze had come down from Canada. We had this big pond that froze. Buffalo carp, forty pounders, swam below, blue shadows sliding under the ice. I bridled Shawnee, a big red Mustang that Uncle'd given me, jumped on bareback. Horses know that ice-walking's for idiots, but I dug heels in and we walked onto the frozen water, cracks zinging out across the deep middle to the other side. There I was, ten feet tall, walking on water. The cracks sang out from me in all directions, energy in motion—humming-bird wings. Over there was the barn where Daddy and I'd slaughtered the wild hog killed last fall, sighted our .30-ought sixes in on a stall door, laying on our bellies a hundred yards off with the blue fall sky cut with persimmon-orange from a tree that's followed me my whole life. I looked at the lightless house, smoke dribbling from the fireplace where Mama was burning the neighbor's Kentucky wood fence for heat, boiling beans, frying potatoes over a woodfire in the fireplace. My brother was inside there, my sisters. The house was built off a curve that high school kids and drunks were always missing, so we'd wake up and somebody's car'd be splattered down the bank across our yard. I straightened my back, breathed a mouthful of frosty Arkansas air, and this howl came up out of my throat. I don't know why, I've never told a soul. By summer, Shawnee'd died, and I had to break his legs to get him in the hole I dug behind the pond levee. The Indian business, the *Red Road* they call it, speaks to some part of me that's hardwired to all that.

Just after Mama died, I went on tour—Florida, Georgia, the Carolinas, and finally Arkansas, the natural state. I was grief-struck, entirely lost. Mama'd started in on me, phones ringing off key at 2 a.m., dream-visions, I believe she was trying her damndest to talk to me from the dead. This guy named Hance ran a sweat lodge, which I knew nothing about, except that maybe you sweat, which made sense—I'd drunk a boatload of vodka since Mama died, and that sort of thing can get you in trouble out on the road. Hance was a sun dancer—whatever that was—and he ran sweat lodges. So I asked for a sweat, and sat outside his house on the scheduled evening, watching the fire pit smoke curl up out of his backyard. Inside, his house had caught fire—something about his wife, leaving a candle burning in a window box that burned up the drapes and a bunch of his childhood pictures, though I didn't know that at the time. "Maybe Mama's followed me here," I said when they told me. It was half joke, but nobody there smiled. Especially not Nicki, a woman he was training to pour water over the rocks, and so run lodge, as he'd been trained to do by a Chief, who, in turn, had been trained by a Chief, who, in turn, had learned the *Red Road* straight from Crow Dog—the Lakota medicine man who'd done time for the Pine Ridge stand-off up near Rosebud. This was the real deal; Hance carried eagle wings, a felony for a white man.

Inside the lodge was like a spaceship in interstellar void, like nothing I'd ever known, like waking dream, like dying. The heat was intense. I thought I really would die, but didn't. And we sang songs in a comforting tongue, words I'd never heard, but somehow knew. The rocks glowed and hissed and popped. My hair was so hot it burned my fingers to touch. After a while, Hance said, "Tell me something about your mother."

"She liked ice water," I said.

Water hissed over the stones, *tunkas,* grandfathers they're called.

Hance crawled around in the dark—I could hear him moving. Nicki sang, *Tunkasila, pilamaya yelo hey.* Her husband beat a drum, *boom, boom, boom.* Hance spit in my face. He beat my head and shoulders with the eagle wings. He blew this shrill bone whistle and the rocks shone with twin eyes. Then he got a coughing fit, terrible. When his breath came back, Hance said, "I think she had a hard time going, not saying goodbye. It was hard for her." I'd grown up around Pentecostals and Baptists, folk who spoke in tongues at revivals, who held healings up by the altar where they made the blind see and the lame walk and the drunkard be sober, who anointed heads with oil and channeled the dead. People bought that bullshit and the offering trays overflowed with wrinkled up dollars. Through Nicki, Hance had asked for thirty-five dollars for this sweat. I guess I got my money's worth—him channeling Mama while she drowned. She liked ice water—she wanted to say *goodbye.*

When we crawled out into the September night near equinox, a light rain falling, I felt clean. Clean in a way that's hard to say: clean from the inside out. And, except for nearly drowning in Hurricane Kyle out off Cape Lookout, North Carolina, and the business of finding all those pictures of Mama and those men while sorting through her bedroom in the house that was Daddy's now, it'd gone mostly okay, my month on the road, the sojourn east to the earth where my people lay buried.

I've agreed to be a Sundance supporter for Nicki. She runs lodge since Hance moved to Mexico. She hosted my vision quest, *hanbleceya*, with a Mandan woman named Evangeline up north—and that's a whole story by itself. Put it this way, you find a spot up on the mountain, build a grave plot for yourself, plant a sapling with colored fabric in each corner, stand there for some days and cry for vision. There's no food and no water, none for you, anyway. What's set out is for spirits; look at it, smell it, it's not for you. At night it's cold and in the daytime it's hot. Forty hours later, I'd have carved off flesh for a drink of water. Something for our kind to remember—when real thirst comes, we'll give anything on earth for one drink of clean water. *Mini Wakan*, the Lakota words, holy water of life.

The cold came on, late, just when the stars emptied, just when the night was about to chew me up and shit me out, a truck groaned through the oat field below, its one headlight going red in the eyes of deer. Evangeline trudged over the dry creek bed, zig-zagging up the path.

"Don't look at me." The words were sharp. "You're dead." She looked me in the face, in the eye. "You're *dead*."

Hearing that you're *dead*, that's a surprise, too. *I'm dead*. The *me* that was *is no more*. I thought to mourn myself, and that was a jolt, like when it's just getting daylight in Utah Spring and you look out the window at the sweet plum that's bloomed overnight, just broken into white blossoms out of the blue. Sun shines and the tree pours it on. Dying's like that, it dawned on me, as Evangeline sang the high, aching funeral song and they hauled my dead ass home.

That night we water the magpie through a medicine dropper. The bird drinks, makes throat noises, and that night I hear him scratching the cardboard box in our basement. In my dreams, the magpie and rattlesnake mix; all you breathing ones, give thanks that snakes don't sprout wings, nor magpies fangs.

By morning, the bird's dead. I drive it up and leave it with a bundle of sage and cedar beside its mate. For all the rest of the week, while I pack for camp, I'm not convinced it was the right thing to have carried the magpie into my basement. Sometimes I mean right and do wrong—who knows the right way to be, how to respond to another living thing? I try, but get it fucked up all the time. *Trust your heart, it can't lie,* Evangeline said before she left me on the mountain. And now, I've agreed to support Nicki during Sundance down on Zuni land in New Mexico. When you support a dancer, when you're there for them at the Sundance, if they get sick or break a toe or go on their period, then the supporter has to step in and dance. That means giving flesh, piercing, the whole nine yards. I've never seen it, and no one's really ever explained it fully to me, but that's what happens. If the dancer you support goes down, you step in and offer your flesh in her place. To be honest, that stops me in my tracks a little, hooking skewers through my chest and hanging from a tree. But that's exactly what I've assured Nicki I'm willing to do, offer flesh.

2.

I drive south, over Soldier Pass and down through Price Canyon where coal seams sparkle. The Book Cliffs were once the continent's west coast, millions of years of sediment washing off the Colorado Plateau until the land started to balloon, forming a dome-shaped anticline eighty miles long and forty wide, the San Rafael Swell where Shamans painted otherworldly anthromorphs on desert varnished cliff faces. By the time I see Sleeping Ute stretched out south and east, something is telling me to take the back way in, from Butler Wash Road along Comb Ridge, twenty miles across the redrock backbone that swells south toward the San Juan River. We stayed here during the Salt Lake Olympics in 2002, me, Jill, Lyra and Moon, drove down to Bluff before the opening ceremonies and rented a two room unit with a kitchenette at Recapture Lodge. Days we'd hike this wash, all the way down to the river once where we walked up on giant *kiva*, a hundred feet across on a raised bank circling the flat mesa on San Juan Hill. Blue sky flung out in all directions. In the perimeter's center, a big river rock, a hundred-pounder, held dark patina from the oils of many hands—the *vulva* rock we called it. Scattered over the hillside, the worn down squares of ancient lodges, pottery, flint and signs of recent prayer offerings. Here is the only corridor through Comb Ridge for eighty miles. All migration must pass here or detour eighty miles into desert, away from the river's life-sustaining waters. A petroglyph of a woolly mammoth shines on a desert varnished wall just upstream; my kind ambushed them here fourteen thousand years ago beneath the giant *kiva*. I picture the blood and feast of slaughter—the *kiva* fires and burnt cedar, all those far off souls singing loudly to the boom of skin drums. The place felt sacred, the huge circle under the blue sky. We found it by pure accident: a February afternoon, getting late, sun sinking into lonely quiet, my wife, daughter and I huddled together around the still-warm vulva stone, Mule's Ear diatreme, the inner-core of an ancient volcano, casting its mile-long shadow downriver.

That was just after 9-11, a few months before Mama died. Truth is, when your mama dies, your own life crashes into a brick wall. It ends then begins—the same goddamn thing. Today I'm driving South toward Zuni land. This second, I'm okay with the world—it seems like the right place to be. I'm supporting a Sundancer, it's started now, a done deal. I'll camp the river tonight, at Sand Island near Bluff. And I've taken the back way in, along Butler Wash, one of the roads we drove while the Olympics played out in Salt Lake—our home not two blocks down from the Stadium where I'd watched tongues of flame burning up from the Olympic Cauldron where a gigantic sign said Light The Fire Within, and a building-sized American flag was hung from the stadium's western side. I pictured a 747 crashing through that flag while everybody sang "God Bless America." The President who was not my President would be there; he'd probably pray over the loud speakers on tv—that smirk somebody needs to knock off his lips. We'd escaped that mess and somehow found Butler Wash Road, drove right up on this mountainous formation shaped like a gigantic ass—that's how I recorded it on my map's notations: *see giant ass.* We found a ruin back there—the three of us, and I've decided to revisit before I sleep.

The way in is a quarter-mile dirt path through cactus, sage and Mormon tea, then a clearing cattlemen use for loading the skittish cows that graze this nook of canyon. A sign warns of the Antiquities Act, to take nothing but pictures, leave nothing but footprints. A year ago floating the San Juan, this guy pocketed a piece of yellow jasper near a giant *kiva*, and not an hour later a thirty-mile-an-hour headwind blew straight into our faces. It howled, bent tamarisk double, was intent—I could feel in my core— on inflicting hurt. Used to be I'd rationalize a piece of painted pottery, a hammer stone, flint chips from a hunting camp. No more. The spring I met Jill coincided with rediscovering an onyx spearhead I found in the Ouachita Mountains as a kid; my brother died that May. I almost buried the thing in the casket with him, but it's still on my desk, always cold to the touch. If rocks have spirits, best leave them alone, take nothing.

In the late-day sun, infolds of the ridge above me hold shadows. The footpath crosses a dry wash where tall grass has died. There's no wind, no noise of any kind save me. This spot on earth, I've walked it once with my wife and daughter on a February afternoon. Now, it has a feel like many eyes watching, a consciousness. The wash banks deepen, cottonwoods on either side and the sign of cattle. A small spring has disappeared. The first ruin, an out-building maybe, just a trace on the ledge to my right—I remember seeing it the first time, thinking it a sign. I walk deep into the narrow canyon, under a barbed wire fence that stretches five feet in the air from one side to the other, laced with green vines—to keep out giants? The quiet is intense. Three times I miss the site, as if it hides, as if you must approach its seam from just the right angle. A thorn buries in my thigh. I snap a few stalks of sage, rub the leaves between both hands and hold them to my face.

Spirit brothers, relatives—permission please. *Aho, mitakuye oyasin.* Sun shines low in the west, right down the spine of the swollen ridge, shockingly beautiful, eighty miles long north to south, a ruddy fenceline for woolly mammoth. Across a river of time humans have bent down and sipped spring water, cupped chill handfuls to their faces, knelt at the grave of a love with pink cliff rose laced into her hair, carried meat dried in a pouch with kidney fat and chokecherry for the long journey home.

I'm lost on the high bank, a formation shaped like a woman's hips, an enormous ass with yawning vulva going dark in the center where boulders have made violence, a place to crawl on hands and knees. I don't know why

I'm here. Idiot me, leaving the tobacco in the truck. I have blue sage. A cricket sings. I could die here and no one would know, not for a long, long time. I've underestimated all things in this life—the medicine, the capacity. I overlook the space between the world and who I am. I have a knife and the sun, the sky above and where I walk. The air is hot. I'm bleeding. Three times I've missed the wash. My heartbeat thrums—the thud-thud swelling my neck. An utter fool alone in the desert, a water bottle sloshes from a carabiner strung to my belt. I filled every container back at Matrimony Spring in Moab. Ever drink that water, I've been told, and you're married to it, betrothed. Holy water beside the Colorado River. *Mini wakan wichi yelo*—holy water of life. Medicine water. *Omakiya yo, help me*, I say and kneel, face the sun, make relatives. To the plant nation, I offer *mini*. To the four-legged and crawlers and winged-ones, water. I plight my troth, pour water. Woolly mammoths walked here. Snake men and spider clan. Together, we speak the language of water. A scarlet gilia, a globe mallow, the gash green and the bloodrose, my water trickles to them and the sky opens and I am home. My brother unhinges jaws; he sips the good spring water. I crawl past the fangs into pure white light.

A juniper throws blue shadow along a slope where the dirt softens below a slight ravine, a path the feet would instinctively walk if there was no path. Up beyond the shade, light pools in a hidden clearing. Dust shines on perfectly masoned walls of time. The air's stone still. I make my way to the level clearing beneath the sharp enclave where the structures are built, cut stone by stone and laid into the rock overhang with an exactness that stuns the bricklayer in me. I enter from the south. A stone viaduct's built exactly where the ancient seep line stains the overhang. Above this, a large room, adjoining another, where charcoal bits, corncobs and shards of unpainted pottery are gathered on flat rocks. The place has suffered since we've been here. Walls have lost distinctness and the granary rooms built into the very back of the overhang have been robbed of their slender cobs. The site's heart is a round *kiva*, about five feet deep, large enough for a dozen people, maybe. Paint layers the inside—yellow, white, black, red—the hues of our species. I imagine starry nights, frost on the cistern, their voices rising. I imagine a thousand years, life and death and the fierce bloodletting of birth here on this earth.

Beyond the *kiva*, laced into the north rim, a two story room with a perfect window is the sharpest remnant of what this place must have been like once. Inside, doorways are stained by the oils of innumerable hands, at the exact places I reach to for support while passing room to room. The fitted stones are woven into the overhang wall, so that I cannot tell where human work leaves off for that of wind and rain. In the room's shadow, the air is cool, grains of it coat my tongue. The sweat is cold on me. Here, at the ruin's highest point, the outside world snaps into focus in a view that blasts out over Butler Wash. I know in a heartbeat that this is the exact spot where mortal danger has been detected. My eyes trace pathways folded into the earth from whence have approached the armed warriors of enemy tribes, waves of locusts and smoke from vast wildfires. From this window, keen eyes would have seen Jill, four-year-old Lyra and me that sunny February day. And a few minutes ago, they would have interpreted and reacted to my clumsy approach. The vision has what I can only describe as a varnish, a holy feel, a *finish*. I crawl down and feel the presence. Vandals have stolen the painted pottery. But they're stupid, all the finest shards have washed down the bank beneath the giant juniper, falling down into the creekbed's mud when hard rains come. They've taken corncobs and points. Somebody's left behind a hunk of green bottle glass—the color of my grandmother's eyes—beside the *kiva* opening. Bottle glass from a broken bottle. *How can people be so goddamn stupid*, that's what I'm thinking, the thought ripping through me, though I ought to know better, my great blind spot. I pick it up, the green bottle glass, feel the smooth edge and put it in my short's pocket, then pick my way through the dirt to the huge juniper. Immediately, I find pottery. The shards are painted in zigzags, red and black squares, geometric angles intersected by concentric lines. The dominant colors are red and black, blood and nighttime.

Wings flap. A horned bird lifts beside me. Straight out of the shadows, it beats the Jesus out of daylight. She lifts into the sunlight, a great horned owl, heavy wings walloping. *Fuck me runnin'*—what Arkansas people say.

Owl. It hits me I've been watched this whole time by a horned owl, her gold eyes seeing me invade her home, pick over the ruins, trespass the corn bins and the *kiva.* She witnessed me stealing the glass. A goddamn owl, she whops air up over the ledge and is gone. Now, I've fucked with an owl. For certain Indians, owl-medicine is the most powerful of all. Some fear it above all things, and others wield the glorious wings, practice the black magic and seek to harm. The cross of owl wings, I saw them this second, sun-splashed. I bushwhack from under her tree, make my way down the ravine, fight the urge to run.

Before I can even start to think the thoughts, link up the implications of what's just happened, I feel them behind my back. If you've ever been trailed by something keen on hurting you, another person, a big cat, something you can't see, but feel, that's what it's like—being stalked. Fear, I taste it, my heart beats fast. I'm not supposed to be here, I don't have permission, I've made a mistake. I've somehow trespassed. I'm leaving as fast as I can, each step quicker than the one before. When I lay fingertip to a neck vein, my heart thuds and I honestly fear a heart attack. Past the dry spring and Antiquities Act sign—take nothing, leave nothing. The thorn burns in my thigh. I get in the truck, start it and turn around, make Butler Wash Road and drive half a mile, maybe a mile, before the right rear tire blows.

When I swing open the Pathfinder's door, an intense wind blows from nowhere, a microburst that nearly rips the rear hatch off its hinges. In an instant, the whole truck's blown full of dirt, this freak wind hurling dust in my eyes. I lift the back seat, remove the jack stand, fit it under a U-joint and crank. I lay on the road underneath the front end, spinning the jack crank when something stings my foot, a scorpion, snake, *Iktome?* The wind is full gale, about to blow the hatch door off my truck—that's what I'm thinking, laying my whole weight into the lugnuts, cranking down the spare. The wind takes my sage, sucks a pair of smudge bundles off my dashboard, the sweetgrass, they vanish. Its voice is rage, malice, means me serious harm. And it is somehow justified. It would be a right thing for the truck to blow off the jack and crush my skull, how can that be? What have I done in this world?

Grit blows under my eyelids. I squint, fit the spare tire onto the bolts, twist each of the six nuts tight with my fingers. The bowl of sky is above and the bowl of earth is below. *Owl wings, bloodstained in the wind*, I wrote the words once for Mama, for the moment she died. One crank on each lug and I'm back inside. The engine catches, fires and I'm moving. Straightaway, the wind dies and the air clears and I see Mule's Ear, the giant gaseous vent that rears on a bend down on the San Juan. I wish for whiskey—I'd damn sure have a drink of whiskey now. My foot's swollen, something with venom has struck me. I make the Mexican Hat highway around eight o'clock, drive down into Sand Island State Park on the San Juan River where one of the longest petroglyph panels on earth culminates in the severed green head—a rare pictograph said to signify the beheaded enemy.

I set camp, then drive six miles to Bluff and call Jill. Our connection's fuzzy, and she doesn't really get what's just happened—the significance of wind and the blowout. The owl slips me altogether. Then my daughter says, "I love you, Daddy," and the old ache hits me in the gut, the fear that I might never see them again.

Back at camp, I limp to the river, bathe and doctor my foot with muddy water. The sun goes. Another day, after I've reached the Sundance grounds and catch my breath, I'll feel the green bottle glass in a front pocket. I'll take it out, hold it glittering under the sun and trace its smoothness. Here is a piece of glass that's seen the river, it's worn that way. The edges are worn smooth. River glass, Raven collects it, lays it in his stash. Owl, too, maybe. As the crow flies, Ass Ruin is twenty miles north. River rafters lose beer bottles to rapids all the live long day. Green is life, green is river, green speaks the language of water. I see it clasped in a leathery claw. *How could I be so stupid?* In my heart, I see it wrapped in razor talons, flown on feathered wings in the mid-day heat. I see her lay it shining inside the painted *kiva* door, on the remains of the ancient altar. What a goddamn jolt, pissing on an electric fence; what horrendous power—truth.

3.

Sunday morning is no time to drive across an Indian reservation, which of course I don't know when I rise early, piss in the river, see coyote drinking over on the Rez side. I hit the road, Highway 191 down into Arizona and the long drive toward Shiprock, seven thousand feet tall, rising like, *well*, a ship out of a desert ocean. I drive due east across the Navajo Nation, over the imaginary line drawn between Arizona and New Mexico. Blue painted hogan doors, east-facing, greet passersby. Time and space come untangled here—for one thing, you can see a hundred miles, I'm guessing a hundred, maybe more, in any direction. My windows are down, the warm dry air in my face. Coffee would be good now. I settle for an orange, peel and bite so juice spurts up on the lens of my sunglasses and I almost plow straight into the cars pulled over for the first wreck.

Flipped on the highway, an American car, a junker Chevrolet—it's flipped and skidded, a football field length gouge carved into the asphalt. Flashing, a half-mile off and hell-bent for leather, the ambulance comes and I've got a front row seat for what happens next. A big-bellied Rez Trooper has already taken a metal saw to the driver's side of the car, cutting off hunks of sheet metal. The ambulance screeches to a stop and out jump three medics with a hand gurney. They run to the flipped car, get on hands and knees and look in through the busted windows. The trooper cuts away. A white man appears from the car's backside. It's clear he was first on the scene—nicely creased shirt sleeves bloody to the elbows. He seems to tell the others what to do, what to expect. Just like yesterday when spirits turned on me, like when Rattlesnake brother unhinged his jaws and Magpie invaded my dreams—how can this be? How on earth? I wonder, with a fresh-peeled orange in my hand.

Cars line up from the other direction. A girl gets out of one, walks up to the car wreck. Her Mama smokes inside the cab of a parked truck. This little girl walks up to the wreck, peeks in, then walks back shaking her head. *No, it's not Daddy,* I read from her lips.

After ten minutes they pull the hugest man I've ever seen out from under the car. Six workers out there now, they roll him onto the gurney, so small it seems silly now. They tighten straps, strain, lift. Veins bulge and they struggle to haul this mammoth man the twenty feet to the ambulance's open back door. They stagger hard left and I'm sure they'll drop him, that this dark haired giant will breathe his last this second in front of my eyes. But the bearers hang tight, they somehow make it. Inside the ambulance, the big man's talking, moving his fingers. He's smiling, telling a joke, pumping a fist. *Yeah!* I hear him scream. Then, siren wailing, the ambulance spins out toward Teec Nos Pos near the state line, and the trooper waves us past the wreckage, back onto the road toward Shiprock.

By the time I can see town, I pass three more wrecks, each one as severe looking as the first. Indians hitchhike all down the highway, some sitting roadside with dollar bills blowing between their fingers. When I stop to pick up an elderly woman with her thumb stuck out, she sees my face, says something in Navajo and bids me leave with a brush of a leathery hand. I leave her there standing in tennis shoes and a flower print skirt, the sun lines cut deep into her face.

The drive from Shiprock south to Gallup is like looking off the earth's curve, a panorama out of a movie, literally, the one where this Indian goes hunting for his father who's burned up in a house trailer—I forget the name, *Smoke Signals?* East seems to fall away forever and more shiprocks sail the red earth, monolithic fins as far as the eye can see. By ten a.m., the heat comes on. I open a can of salty peanuts, fish an icy lemonade from the cooler behind the driver's seat. Jill wrapped two turkey sandwiches for my lunches. I find the first one beside the lemonade, unwrap the foil and eat—turkey and Muenster, lettuce, fresh tomato—cold, cold, it's the best sandwich I've ever tasted, on the road to Sundance, green bottle glass from the spirit world in my right pocket. I don't know where I'm going. Time unwinds, clean dry air blows in my face and I eat, a day and a half from my last drink of alcohol, I'm thinking about that, how this dry-out week is good medicine, a great good thing. The hitch in my side has faded and the loneliness, leaving my wife and daughter to drive seven hundred miles to a camp full of strangers up to who knows what, the foolish, foolish feeling for doing that, for blowing my tire out in a place where the elements could have killed me, wandering miles of rattlesnake washes for no reason at all, unsettling owls and watching a full-grown man get cut out of a car, why on earth would anybody come this way, that's how I've been feeling, like I'm throwing my life away, tossing it up in the wind and letting it blow where it may.

This is Sunday, and anybody who ever thought about selling tires in Gallup, New Mexico is home with their family scrambling eggs and frying bacon. In the one auto parts store that's open, an Indian guy smiles and shakes his head when I ask where's a Goodyear. "Frank's, down the road on the right," he says. "He's not there. Maybe Monday," he says, turns back to the tv ball game on the counter.

I use a gas station bathroom, fill up and buy ice for the coolers. "Do you know how to get to Zuni," I ask the attendant.

"That way," she says, points. "Go straight."

That's how I go, ten-thirty now, I head south toward Zuni land with seven gallons of spring water, a star blanket and pictures of Jill and Lyra and a notebook where—scribbled at sixty-five miles an hour—is the line I've sought for *Go Love*, the novel I've written for two years now: *Barely home, we head West*, the pivot to the third and final move. Backseat, in a silver pail, I carry the vision quest bundle, tangibles that I managed to bring back from the mountain—sage, cedar and a heartful of fear. The sun is good today, the warm air sweetened with a taste of pinyon. The land begins to rise, cedar with long aching views, and the first of one whole hell of a lot of turquoise trading posts: BUSSES WELCOME, they all say, BEST TURQUOISE IN THE WEST. ZUNI MADE. WILL TRADE FOR ANYTHING.

Near Black Rock I head East on 53 where a sign says *Visit El Morro National Monument—See Inscription Rock.* I skirt the Zuni River through Pescado and Ramah, where the first wolf refuge signs appear. Ramah is small, quaint, near the shady bend of a river where I think to fish some day. A museum is open there, built of red stone. I stop at the one restaurant. Inside an Indian girl looks five minutes for keys before walking me out to the freezer, keying the padlock, and lifting out two bags of crushed ice. I drink another lemonade, pee in the parking lot for some stupid reason—people inside can see me plain as day—head on through town and turn south at BIA 125 where the sign says *Come Visit The Wolves: Candy Kitchen Rescue Ranch.* My gut tells me I'm near ceremony—the hair on the back of my neck stands. The sign repeats every few miles, along with *Mini-Ranch For Sale* signs and a little town called Mountain View where orange-dressed inmates from the town jail hammer a house frame together in an open field. No one looks at me when I drive past. Their tools echo off the monolithic slab.

I miss Great White Father Road—Great White Father Road?—and end up at the wolf refuge where I immediately whomp my forehead on the hogan door header.

"I'm lost," I say.

A pretty woman, blue eyes glittering behind a sun-lit counter, looks me over. She recognizes me, I can tell, as one of the White Indians. I passed my turn many miles back. "The best way to tell you," she says. "Just look for a junked van—no wheels, no windshield." She smiles. I smell wolf. "It's a real piece of shit. That's your road." Photographs of sassy-eyed wolves and wolf-dogs detail each wall—Shadow, Zeus, Loki, Ishi, Wambli, Raven, their names are written underneath toothy smiles. Outside, they pace inside tall chain-link fences. Tours begin at 11, 1 and 3. Two wild packs nearby—the northern and southern—are blood relations to the penned animals. A nailed up sign says, "Sleep with wolves howling under starlit skies."

I drive to the junked van, up the rough road to a high pinyon mesa and the Cougar Ranch sign strung between twin spruce posts. Two long-haired men joggle in the cab of a truck in front of me—yarn-wrapped smudge sticks on the dashboard. I smell woodsmoke, see the shine of windshields parked amongst pines, the flash of tent fabric in the thickets. Feet stick out the propped open camper door of the truck I park beside. I open the door, the heat full on me now. My stomach sinks—I could vomit any second. My last chance to avoid this cup passes. Trees are strung with hoops and leg bones: all down a path to the Sundance grounds the limbs of dead trees flutter.

Entering a ceremony is like walking into a holy roller revival during a healing when everybody's speaking in tongues and a half-dozen copper-heads are being passed around while a live rock band onstage gets down on "I'm in the Gloryland Way." That's how it feels, when you come from the outside, drive up upon a people who've lived many days and nights under the sky, known the lodge fire, breathed burnt sage and cedar, made offer-ings and sang holy songs, summoned spirits and performed magic rites laced with blood and smudge fanned by eagle wings. I remember when Jill and Lyra drove up on ceremony in Utah where I'd worked a vision quest camp for four days; women had to wear skirts and smudge off before setting foot on the property. I was fireman that day, forking coals, restacking the twenty-eight stones for the lodge that Hance was apt to call any second. A man with two black crows tattooed on his chest walked up and said "Your lady's here."

Sure enough, there came Jill and Lyra in the Pathfinder. They got out in shorts. Lyra was chewing a popsicle. The day before we'd put three on the mountain, built their graves with tobacco prayer ties. They'd be thirsty by now, the thirtieth hour, dying. "Put on a dress," I told my wife and began smudging the truck. Jill looked at me, and then uphill to Vision Quest camp, which was a sort of lockdown commune where everyone wore either a skirt or long pants, no sunglasses, and kept referring to brothers and sisters dying on the mountain, feeding real food and water to the fire to sustain them. She shook her head and rifled a suitcase. "This is crazy," Jill said, and jerked out a sundress and a skirt for Lyra. "I can't believe this," she said, fighting tears. She spoke the truth. *Crazy—that's* how it feels, walking into ceremony.

I park and walk up a dirt path to the kitchen where a big man stacks number ten cans of peaches into a wood cupboard. Nicki and her husband, a mailman in real life, stand outside where the chowline will be—they look dazed. Mailman says, "Michael." They've just got here, are about to set camp. Nobody's in charge, that's clear. Nicki hugs me, looks me in the face. A Utah beauty, she's let her hair go elder white. "Thank you." She says it, looks at the ground. Nicki's fifty-five, ex-Mormon.

Two hundred yards downhill, shirtless men toil in 106 degree heat. Smoke from the lodge fire rises—wisps twisting upward. In the kitchen, a woman's voice—down home south—comes out of a man's mouth; he's dressed like a clown—hair tight on a skull shaped like the drawings I've seen of Neanderthal—high forehead, tremendous jaws, set on a thin, delicate body, striped pants ballooning from thigh to ankle. He's talking to the big man stacking peaches, rolling vowels. "Way-el," he says. "I'll show take care uh him." He lifts a green snake, thumb and index finger behind the diamond-shaped head. A rattler, I can tell from the angry buzz. The woman-man from the southern wild walks off to the bushes dangling the green rattlesnake between fingers. It's one o'clock. For ceremony protocol, I've pitched my sunglasses so the light and heat are ferocious.

Under a tall pine overlooking the entirety of the Sundance grounds, I make camp. I align the tent mouth east, unroll my bag and set house. Jill and Lyra's picture go in the net meshing still bloodstained from where I split my head open in Utah's San Rafael Swell the Memorial Day weekend before Mama died, when I was half-crocked and somehow managed to fall down and crack my skull by the fire, then wander down to the tent where Jill and Lyra lay sleeping. And Jill's not good with blood, it makes her sick, so me gushing like that all over the place was too much. She retrieved a friend from across camp and the two of them did what they could. Next morning, I woke up without a clue until I stuck three fingertips into the wound, a "full-through laceration," the doctor who sewed fourteen tight stitches into my head said. I remember crawling out of the tent, wandering up to the camp kitchen, the first one of our group of twenty or so out of bed. I scooped up blood from beside the sharp rock, threw it behind bushes. Then, idiot to the end, I put on a ballcap and cooked the whole lot scrambled eggs and ham, hash brown potatoes. Later, after I'd driven two hours into Green River and called 911 to interrupt the town doc's Sunday school lesson, the medics met me outside the emergency clinic doors with grim looks. "Where is he? The guy with the head wound?" they asked.

I took off the ballcap. "It's me," I said. If it had been a joke, that was the moment for the punch line, only there was none. I could have died. They looked at me like people awaiting a punch line.

While the doctor sewed, he went on about things like lock-jaw and encephalitis, how the rock had cut a gash clear into my skull. Many times I've wondered how it would have been for Jill and Lyra to get up and find me dead, to have to lay a tarp over my face and carry that death grimace in their minds for the rest of their lives. I've thought on that, what that would be like for my daughter, my baby, to bury me in a hole and say goodbye forever, and keep coming to that hole month after month, year after year, or not. I've wondered why I didn't die, or thought maybe I did die and inhabit some kind of dream now, or an alternate universe, or that Mama somehow intervened and gave her life for mine that night while I lay gushing blood by the sharp rock beside the fire. A month later she was dead, and that's what got me into all this—running from her ghost, the healing sweat lodge, hitting the red road.

I lash my vision quest blanket's four corners to the tent roof, then walk down the slope toward work. Sunlight rips through my eight-pointed star—red, yellow, green, blue, white, colors of the ghost way.

4.

An ant hill arrests me. Fire ants erupt from the mouth, they radiate. A pinyon circle, six feet across, is built around the hill where bits of cloth and foodscrap scatter. Somebody's feeding these ants. Big red drones carry hunks of watermelon rind, macaroni, red, yellow and brown M&Ms, a balogna wrapper. All down the dirt path to the dance grounds the ant hills are like this, cones encircled by cloth-wrapped pinyon larded down with M&M's, rib bones, honeydew rind. And the trees, come to think of it, bones are strung from the limbs of certain cedars and pinyon, especially the dead ones. Antlers, femurs, half a dainty ribcage dangle from the limbs of a dead tree. I get my first whiff of the outhouse, then the fire. A chainsaw rips hell out of a thicket to the north. I walk downhill on a dirt road wide enough for three trucks. The path goes through a gate that swings off a rude fence, past a shack built of cedar planks where a long-haired man sits stone-faced with a pitchfork between his legs. Two *inipis*—sweat lodges—sit blanket-covered at the mouth of the only open pit fire in the state of New Mexico. Straightaway east, dead center of a soccer field sized circle, a dead tree is wrapped with what I'll learn are twenty-thousand prayer ties, glistening bundles that vine up fifty feet into the withered branches.

Before sundancing, one must have *the dream*. Mine came on a full moon night, the eve of *hanbleceya*, sleeping just outside the Sundance grounds on Toone land in Croyden, Utah. I dreamed myself dancing; under a full Buck

Moon, I walked out and touched the tree and it felt like flesh. My daughter Lyra slept just beyond the circle—would these dreams trace the blanks behind her shut eyes? I touched the ropes, pulled one taut so high leaves shook. These twisted cords, tied to the highest bough, shone in the moonlight. Higher up, bundled, human flesh, tied with ribbons, twisting this way and that, floating under Moon's sway. That's how my dream went—no drums booming, just me in the dark that became light.

Now, in the circled arbors, helpers staple sun block tarps onto roof joists. A bare-chested man in a brown fedora assigns my first job, building stilts under the camp water cistern, a two-hundred-fifty gallon container sloshing on top of a wooden spool—the big-ass rickety kind you can steal off any construction site. Charley, the guy who gives me the job, meets me at the dancefloor ground. He holds out a big rough hand, says, "I am thankful for your prayers."

In ceremony, people are always saying things that would sound insane anywhere else—get used to it. "We're thankful for your prayers," he says again.

Pinyon sap scents the woodsmoke. The long-haired man with a pitchfork doctors the fire, forks air to the coals. Charley's eyes are milky-blue, the color of a sailor's or witchdoctor's ; with these eyes, he could fake blindness, hold out the fedora and prophesy you out of your last coin.

A bundle of white sage, criss-cross wrapped with black and white thread burns in Charley's right hand. "Here," he says.

I spread my arms for *azilia*. "You need some help?"

He purifies my face, right shoulder, over the length of my right arm and down my legs, back up the same way on the left side to my face; then I turn around and he makes the same clockwise rounds, only I lift each foot for him to pass the sage under. His chest is scarred either side just above the nipples, bulges like stray navels.

"Hell yes," he says. "You asking?"

Charley's tall, six-two or three, maybe, and he's got that poor mouth look of people who never darken a dentist's doors. That glint in his eyes I'll see over and over here. He's dreamed the eagle dream, I'll learn, so his

56

pilgrimage to Zuni land involves skewering wooden hooks through his shoulders front *and* back, tying one end of the ropes to the hooks and the other to a crossbar they'll affix to the new tree, where he'll be hoisted for the eagle flight. If you have this dream, of being an eagle, keep it to yourself, that's what I say. His supporter's already said *no way in hell* is he stepping in for that. *No way, Jose.* Charley walks me up to the kitchen tent, tips the fedora toward the water tank, puts his shoulder into it so the whole business heave-hoes. "Here she is," he says. "You fix her?"

"Sure."

Charley gives me a cordless drill, the very worst kind, and a handful of five inch screws. I know the battery's worn down before I ever pull the trigger. This guy who introduces himself as Florida Boy intervenes with a twenty-eight ounce Plumb hammer and a box of sixteen-penny nails, a handsaw, steel stakes and an eight-pound sledge. We break into a mess of two-by-fours and go to town, tack kickers to the spool and brace the suckers with stakes driven a good foot into Zuni dirt. Each hammer report *shrings* across the grounds; I imagine green rattlesnakes lifting triangular heads, flicking their little tongues and tasting our sweat.

"Flesh offering," Florida Boy says when I lay my leg open on a stake head.

"Where you from."

"Florida, don't you know." His face breaks into this big dumb grin, that hides something. "Otherwise I'd be Georgia Boy or Maine Boy or somewhere else boy."

"You?" He leans a stiff shoulder into our work. Rock solid, the cistern doesn't budge. "Nice," he says.

"Arkansas. Utah now."

"I was in Arkansas onest." He opens the spigot and pours two coffee cups full of cool well water. "My Uncle lives there. A place called Bauxite where they got these blue holes."

"Mine, too," I say. The water is good—clean with a metallic bite.

Florida Boy's here to support a dancer from Melbourne, Florida, just across the Indian River from the barrier island where Jill's people live. He's volunteered to man the kitchen, which is usually taboo for a man at these Indian ceremonies. Jill had simply shit, that first time at Vision Quest camp, having to wait hand and foot on any man hankering for a bologna sandwich. "Can I have another cup of coffee, sweets?" they'd ask, or "How about a tad more of that pie?" and I'd feel her glare from a hundred yards off.

The snake handler walks up arm-in-arm with a little intense looking man whose beard is intricately trimmed. He tips a curt brown bowler, and some wind gets into his blousey pants. "Red Wolf," he says, nods his head, so all those earrings get the sun. "Look. Flesh offering." He points to my cut shin, the blood running down into my sandal. Then he fills a kettle, lights a camp stove burner and makes tea. "Thanks for the hep," Florida Boy says, and I can tell he means it.

Back at my tent, I dress the wound. The photograph I've brought of Lyra looks like Mama, the big, broad confident smile, the honest sweetness in her eyes. Jill teaches special education, long, long days in classrooms where the faces of the presidents shine above blackboards and *fuck you* dictionaries—the new titles scrawled across the spines. I've kept her school pictures year-by-year since 1986, the year we met, when I ran off to Washington, D.C., to live with her. On a field trip to the National Air and Space Museum, all her touched first graders screamed "Mr. Fish! Mr. Fish! Take us to the gravity room." I roll a cigarette, gulp down an ice cold lemonade. The big pine I've chosen is good, a strong windbreak, cool shade, a sappy Christmas smell. Early arrival has given me the highest spot in Sundance camp. Thirty feet north, a cabin tent's staked. Sleeping bags and Thermarests are rolled up inside the insect net vestibule, though clearly, nobody's home.

By afternoon, the place is dusty with arrivals. Here's what they see: turn off of Great White Father Road and drive into Cougar Ranch. The rough road climbs steeply west onto dry mesa. People are following fucked up maps—so they're not sure where they are. Like Florida Boy, travelers converge here from all over—Wisconsin, New Jersey and the whole East Coast, London, England, Peru, Japan, China. Eskimos are here. Like me, many have driven all the way to the Candy Kitchen Wolf Compound, whomped their foreheads on the hogan's low doorjamb and shouted *goddamnit* at the blue sky. The woman's blue eyes glittered. Disorientation is ingrained on the consciousness out here in Zuni, the angles seem out of kilter—just the slightest bit, no shit. And we're all sober as judges, though I doubt judges have ever been sober. But lord, god *we* are, sober to the hilt. Folks are a little messed up by their sobriety when they roll in here, straight for maybe the first time in a good long while. This is Mecca for fuck-ups, according to Red Holy, anyway. Our Sundance chief, True Heart, is a recovering addict. When he was in Korea, they made him do awful things, and when he got back he got all screwed up on booze and pills. Ceremony saved his life, he says, and these white film makers made a documentary film on his road to recovery in South Dakota. Now True Heart has a Master's Degree and is a professional counselor. What I'm saying, this dance is for the afflicted, addicts and drunks clinging to sobriety by ties less tenuous than flesh. I'm well into day two—forty hours dry now. Any minute this place will be overrun with drunks and addicts—a tribe of freaks and lunatics who'll recognize me at once, no goddamn doubt, as their long lost white brother.

Car windows and windshields begin to flash—that's the first sign that you're close, the glare. Then there's the woodsmoke and the kitchen where down home boys in skirts hold green-headed rattlesnakes, and one sure steady supported mother of a water tank shines kickers in all directions. Sitting on a cooler under my shade tree, peroxide bubbling down my leg, I smoke two hand-rolled cigarettes and watch them arrive on the bumpy road. To an outsider, say somebody here fresh from Lonoke County, Arkansas, these White Indians would be about the weirdest bunch of people imaginable, like Burning Man Mormons, Buddhist Monks, Pentecostals and island cannibals, Moonies, Hare Krishnas, and Jim Jones mixing up the Kool-Aid down in Guyana, all that. Of my own free will I've joined a camp full of insane freaks about to do unspeakable violence to themselves and others. A wave of nausea goes through me and I think to pack my shit and drive out of here, go back to my wife and daughter and garden and soft-bed-summertime. A big white car with tinted windows and a veterans bumper sticker eases up past the kitchen and halfway down the dirt ruts to the Sundance compound. When the back lid pops, a trunkful of fresh sage shines. I haul a dripping ziplock out of the icy cooler and eat Jill's second sandwich, relish the cool cucumber with a hint of salt and mayonnaise.

On my way down to the fire, a man steps from the white car. A Lakota, I can tell, he's shorter than me, stocky, grey hair falling over his shoulders. When I'm close, he looks me straight in the eye, and his eyes are kind eyes—the sort you recognize in a second. "True Heart," he says and opens his arms wide as if he knows me, as if he's waited a long time for me to walk up to his trunk.

Red Holy claims that True Heart's got these awesome powers—that he can make the lame walk and the blind see, that he can shapeshift and walk on air. Chief sees into your heart's heart, knows things straight away that even you don't know. The Chief, Red Holy says, is liable to walk up to you and ask you to join the dance, to pierce yourself for the people. It happens every year, Red Holy says, True Heart walks up to somebody, reads them and asks them and next thing they know they're dancing in a red skirt—it's part of the deal, part of being here. It's how Red himself got called into the dance. And if you've had the dream, the dream of dancing beneath the Tree of Life, why True Heart's sure to sniff that out straightaway. "Best take your moccasins," Red said after our last sweat.

I say my name into the ears of the Sundance Chief. "I've heard good things about you," I say.

He nods, shakes my hand with both his hands. "*Wash tey,*" he says, *thank you.*

"I'm with the Utah people."

"Good." He looks me in the face. He reads my heart. A drinker can spot another drinker from a mile away—the thin cheek skin where veins show through, tiny blood webs that flare when the body ingests hot peppers, whiskey or fried fish. Our faces get this blown out look. The eyes are blank slates, impossible to read. Forget all the bullshit about tremors and slurring and stagger-down fits. Truth is, drinkers are often the steadiest, most articulate, seemingly balanced actors in the whole scene—geniuses at reconcil-ing the heart and mind. Maybe True Heart sees me through straightaway. Veins spangle his own cheeks. Maybe he has pity.

Nicki has been asked to sew him a star blanket for ceremony; I've seen it, Uwipi colors—yellow, white, black, red, a perfect quilted star, zig-zags for *wakinyantanka*, the thunder beings, *from your Utah relatives* sewn in fine red cursive. "Good to meet you," True Heart says. "I welcome you to this place."

I say "Thank you," and hesitate. We are wrapped in the aroma of sweet sage, cedar, the woodsmoke rising from the east. I'm forty-four and one-half years old, a long goddamn haul down the road from where I started. His eyes are on me as I walk through the Sundance gate.

5.

The only open-pit fire in the state of New Mexico is being tended by a North Carolinian whose blood-shot eyes testify to three nights without sleep. "They won't leave me alone," he says, under the shade of the fireman's shed. Out in front of us, men work the Sundance arbor, stapling up shade cloth. That's another thing about ceremony, the work's ballbreaking, just unbelievable, really. You work yourself to death, sleep like a baby at nighttime.

"It's a lot of work," I offer.

Fireman looks at me through bloodshot blue eyes. He looks like a poet, somebody I've listened to spill their guts for three hours straight on a barstool. His voice is gruff—a smoker's. "Uh uh," he says. "The work's no problem. I love this work."

I'm sitting in the blue chair beside him. "Who is it that won't leave you alone?"

"Spirits." He says it straight-faced, lights a cigarette. "They're hammering me this second."

A white-haired man walks into the fire lodge, says, "Thank you firemen. Thank you for all you do." He shakes both our hands, grabs an armload of blankets and walks back out.

"Now you're a fireman," fireman says. "The only shift open's from midnight till six. You good on that?"

Before I can answer, he says, "Good."

"I guess so."

"Good. I'm from Asheville. The Bible Belt," he says. "And we got five sweat lodges on my street alone."

"In Asheville?"

"Yeah," he says. "I do rehab work—DWI's, that kind of stuff. And I work with people whose Kundalini energy has showed up. People get the shit scared out of them when their Kundalini shows up."

"Kundalini?"

Fireman looks some place way off, past the dance circle and the dead tree where a pajama-dressed man performs *tai chi*—contorting himself inconceivably. A wooly buffalo blanket is rolled in the corner with seven mammoth skulls. "It's energy," he says. "From earth's core."

I've brought three ounces of hand rolling tobacco—good stuff. The natives use it as a holy plant whose roots sink into earth and whose smoke rises in air as prayer. *Canupa wakan,* the holy pipe, to smoke is to pray. These White Indians smoke the Jesus out of tobacco. I roll, smoke.

Fireman lifts his pitchfork, winces. "Midnight till six," he says.

The wolves kick in late—a sound that touches my spine. The Buck Moon's near full, the fire pops, a whirl of sparks hissing, rising. I hear two packs, east and southwest—the way home. One's voice is *wakan*, wholly distinct, a sound like no other. This voice rings my bell, speaks my self, is the most *deeply* real talk that has ever come into my head. It anchors and buoys, fractures then coalesces. *Pieces of eternity*, the poet said, the howling of wolves. And here *I* am. Of all things, *me*. I tend the ceremonial fire. Under a July Buck Moon, shadows and light ghost-skitter off the world's dark lip. The wolf's voice swerves the Milky Way, the curved sky's bones. *Ska-ska,* the people say, *great mystery, great great mystery*. There's part of me that's a stranger to myself, though I've sniffed its trace my whole life. Fireside, the barked notes stun.

Two willow-framed sweat lodges are covered with blankets and tarps at my back, the door flaps open. I learned the Lakota way to build *inipi* one frosty December near winter solstice. A piece of earth is chosen, prayed over. The making relatives ceremony is offered to the plant nation, to the animal nation. Tobacco is offered. Every attempt is made to do things in a good way. Green willows are found growing on a river bank—they smell like medicine and the leaves shimmy in a breeze. Prayer and tobacco is offered and thirty-three *willow people* are harvested and brought to the site where the *inipi* will be built. One willow stake is driven into what will be the inner pit, where water will be poured over the *tunkas*, grandfather stones, earth's eldest. A length of rope is looped round the stake and a circle is scribed into the earth, eleven feet or so in diameter. The rope is stretched west through what will be the *inipi* door and another stake is hammered to mark the altar, three feet outside the doorway. Eight feet further west, another stake is driven into the heart of the fire pit.

Earth from the inner rock pit is placed around the second stob to form an altar that will stand outside the *inipi* door, the inverse of inside. Sixteen holes are crow-barred around the pit, tobacco and prayer sifted into each. A fire is laid. Sometimes the willows are skinned, so their white flesh shines. In winter, the willows are limbered over fire and medicine gets in the air. Then, west to east, in a moment when no one speaks, the right willow is chosen and a serpentine curve is bent over the hips and back. If it cracks, strips of cloth and prayer are wrapped around the injury. A second willow is bent from the east and when the curve is right, the two are bound together in the middle forming a squat oval. A twin arch is bent beside the first, and the whole process is repeated north to south making a medicine wheel cross. Two more double-arches are tied at forty-five degree angles to this cross; inside the frame, the sixteen willows conjoin in a perfect eight-pointed star, the same as one finds on star blankets. Three full hoops are tied clockwise around the structure, and a fourth is added for healing. A west facing door is bent in an upside down U, and outside the door a willow is embedded in the altar; stripped of bark, bear claws, talons, strips of holy cloth are tied here, along with the blotched plumes of *Wanbli Gleska*—the immature bald eagle.

Behind me, doors yawn open. That solstice, before the *inipi*, I was asked to dig a four-foot hole into the center of the already dug fire pit. Workers gathered in a circle around the fresh dug dirt. Solstice: the sun stood still. From a plastic grocery bag—the sort you get at the Piggly Wiggly check-out—a golden eagle, new-dead and plucked of plumage, was passed down, set facing the lodge door, then buried, and on top of this, stones followed by fire. I watched a sincere white man lay a golden eagle into a leg-deep hole beneath a fire pit. All through the sixteen-door lodge, I couldn't quit thinking of it down there, a felony, a goddamn golden eagle. Months later, a chief got wind of this eagle lodge and it was dug up and burned.

Behind me this second, two medicine lodges, one for men and one for the women who'll sweat two rounds into the spirit world before sunup, then walk the circumference of the Sundance arena, entering from the east with the rising sun. Two more rounds close each day. Inside, during these last rounds, they'll be offered medicine, chokecherry juice and sage tea. Moonlight will shine through the doorway and the wounded dancers will sit on forgiving earth. The stones will glow and some will see spirits, *Iktome Zee,* yellow spider. They will bleed and pray and say *mitakuye oyasin, all my relations.* I am related to all things and all things are related to me. I sit on the fire pit's lip and breathe and listen to wolves. This is how it is to be human, tending night fires that burn above bones. How much to remember? How much to forget?

My co-fireman is a lawn and garden tractor salesman from St. Louis. He shows up at the fire, red coals shining in the glasses frames where each eye should be. He sits down and we don't say a lot, though he tells me he's come from St. Louis with Roberto, that he started sweating about six months ago, that the Sears model I owned back in Arkansas had to have been the heavy-duty unit, since I was able to bushhog my side pasture. I haven't seen him in the light yet, and, for my money, it's tough to trust somebody first met in dark.

North of the fireman shed, wood is stacked in chest-high cords. I choose a smallish chunk, lean it into a log that's gone to coals and pitchfork holes for oxygen. My first night, morning now—tree day. I've heard about it, the ceremony that begins all.

Out of the dark walks a bare chested man who sits cross-legged in front of the fire, begins to play a wooden flute. Grey hair flows down his bare back. I give him room. His notes mix in and out of the wolf song, and when the fire catches I can see how the light filters through his hair, around the edges his shoulders make in the dark. Jill, my wife, she plays the flute, and I've always admired that, making music with breath. I recognize him as Charley—the man who thanked me for my prayers and gave me the job fixing the water cistern on the rickety wooden spool this morning. The flute-notes whistle over blue and yellow flames. The sky is delirious—a dream. I see the hummingbird myth above, how angered Creator once threw a blanket over all existence and hummingbird was sent from the animal world to make starholes with her beak. The Hubble Space Telescope once photographed a piece of empty sky, a dark pinpoint near Cassiopeia, shutters wide open for thirty unblinking days. The developed photograph, blown-up to the size of a living room, was displayed at the World Space Symposium, where, clear as a conjurer's ball, ten thousand galaxies—spirals, ellipticals, barred and irregulars—shone where before was not one goddamn thing. Mama, my mother, flown through the Milky Way, and beyond: where the dead go, is there love? Part of me is here for her, Mama. In a story I've heard called "The Lame Shall Enter First," the child Norton is told that his dead mother has gone into the sky he witnesses through an attic telescope. That's where his father finds him, the noose tight around the boy's neck, feet dangling from a rafter where he's made the leap to find his Mama—the root of all quests. The truth? Ten thousand galaxies in a pinpoint of darkness? If nothing else, the sky alone should blow our heads off.

Charley breaks into a ragged version of "Amazing Grace." And he doesn't stop when he misses a note. The wolves quiet, the fire dies down and Charley's "Amazing Grace" goes from bad to downright awful. The whole goddamn universe is flying apart in all directions, just hauling ass every which way, and still Charley plays on. I'm embarrassed for him. I remember the funereal voices bawling on a fake green carpet laid over Bermuda grass, under the blue tent arbor where Mama's casket sat on a silver scaffold, fiercely radiant in the Arkansas heat—

When we've been there ten thousand years, bright shining
as the sun, we've no less days to sing God's grace, than when we
first begun.

I'm grateful when Charley stops.

"I've worn out many moccasins," he says, "in thirty years of this." He passes his hand over the fire. "Thank you for loving the fire. You are fireman above, but there's a fireman below. Right down there," he says and points into the fire.

The lawn and garden man's eyes are all lit up, really, the flame dancing in his glasses.

"And the fireman below, he can only keep the fire as well as you do up here. I've had the privilege to light this fire for three years now. We must honor the fireman below or this whole dance can't happen." He points into the fire. Like all the rest of us, his voice is a smoker's voice, a husky rasp. He's gaunt, maybe heroin once. And a vet, Vietnam, I'll learn. "There," he says. "That fire's your teacher now."

Charley rises, walks off into the dark.

After he's gone a few minutes, the co-fireman says, "That was the most mystical moment of my life." His eyeglass shines. "Incredible," he says.

The wacky West: I've seen grown men mow their grass in spring snowstorms. A family of river otters swimming single file, tossing a skull upward, then snatching it between teeth—their play-time ball. One of the cemetery deer across our street, a doe, was run over in front of my house, belly full of fermenting crabapples from the University where I teach. I butchered her, wrapped her in freezer bags written over with names like *arm roast, neck stew, backstrap butterflies, 2005*. A magical moment?

"Do we both *have* to be here?"

"No," he says. "I'll stay."

I agree to take his place at 4:30 a.m., stumble uphill to my tent and sleep.

6.

I have lived for sunrises, mornings writing in the cold study I've built onto our house, east-facing, first light pinkening the Oquirrhs when day comes. This morning on Zuni Land in New Mexico, 18 July—a Monday—two days from full moon with the lone wolf howling in the north, I'm fireside, wrapped in a lodge blanket. The lawn and garden man has left our fire sweet—hot coals, little flame. Fire is ground zero for ceremony, someone must tend it every second. I remember looking down from the mountain during my vision quest, sparks rising, and taking great comfort that someone would be there all night, that this fire would devour the food and water that my daughter offered to keep me strong. After every lodge, before feasting, someone feeds the fire. When the fire's over, ceremony's over. Earth, air, fire and water—of these, fire alone can be made by human hand. Fire is our kind's twin—our births coincide. A friend conjures it with a stringed bow and spindle. He sprinkles cedar shake, says the fire prayer. The transcendent moment is combustion, when we stand on two legs and walk away from our primate kith and kin, armed with the holy ghost fire. Our whole show starts and ends with fire. Fire made gods of us.

I'm joined. He sits to my left, cups woodsmoke to his chest. "Nice work," he says. "You been out here all night?"

"Since 4:30."

"Good fire," he says. "I got here last night late. With my daughter."

"Mine's home. My daughter. I miss her."

"Where's home."

"Utah. Salt Lake City. You?"

The sky lightens so the big bear fades and the visible planets grow indistinct, Saturn, Jupiter with four moons on its shoulders. Way up behind us, on the tree covered hill, a light snaps on, Florida Boy making coffee, draining water from the braced cistern. "I come over from Colorado. My son and wife's at home."

"You know somebody here?"

He smiles, says, "Dad's here."

There's just enough light to make out the features I saw yesterday in the face of the Sundance chief—the wide forehead and honest smile.

We shake.

"I tied a new drum last week and brought it to try. Hell, I started not to come, but I'm glad I did. It's good to be by the fire like this. To come and pray this way." He says, "Thank you," and walks off toward the kitchen. Then I'm alone with the fire for a while until Red Wolf materializes out in the Sundance theater, doing Tai Chi beneath the tree as the sun rises and the day begins to thrum.

"How'd you like your eggs?" The voice is behind my back, feminine, the southern drawl I've heard roll off the lips of the angry women I grew up loving.

"Any way's fine," I say. "Who *are* you?"

"Do you know what *winkte* means?" He nods his head the way my people do to signal that we're in agreement, we all know Lakota here.

I say I don't.

"An adult homosexual male," he says. "You can't have Sundance without a *winkte*. You can call me *winkte*." A while later he serves me eggs over-easy, bacon and wheat toast, hot coffee, and I am grateful.

After breakfast, Sundance Chief calls all dancers into a circle just north of the sweat lodges, maybe thirty feet from the fire. True Heart's son has hauled down a huge kettle drum—the *boom, boom* like heartbeat. Someone sings. And the circle grows—the first formal gathering of this year's Sundancers.

True Heart is here, his face full of sun—he holds a hand up, begins to speak.

"Someone asked," he says, "Why do we do this? What is the purpose of the Sundance? I ask you dancers, you've come a long way, some of you, spent a lot of money to get here. The best way I can say it is like this."

The voice is strong—his eyes look you straight, they hesitate, say I know—*my light sees your light.* He bends his arm at the elbow, so the forearm and hand, the splayed fingers reach straight up to the blue sky. It's hot, dry—I stand with sixty of the oddest folk I've witnessed, though not really. When I was a kid, Mama got Jesus. She was all the time dragging us to full gospel revivals where people committed glossolalia very, very loudly, where it was not uncommon for a preacher to anoint someone's head with oil, and them fall outright on the floor and writhe in epileptic fits, then the snakes would be brought out by a one-legged man and the electric guitars would all screech feedback from hidden amplifiers. *Mama,* I'd think, *why on earth?* But there we were, looking for something, just like everybody else. This is nothing like that—these people aren't scary—though that dead tree standing out behind us on the dance ground, fifty-some ropes dangling down like hangman's nooses, that's wicked scary. Up there, skeins of fabric blow from one bundle that's wrapped like a newborn, tied to a high limb. Flesh and blood, that's what this tree is about. The bundle worries my heart, it grinds me fine.

"The best way I know, it's like this. Think of the sunflower." His arm, his hand, is a sunflower, fingers blooming red and gold. "The sunflower moves with the sun." The flower-hand moves across the sky, follows the sun's motion. "The sunflower moves with the sun. All day long it moves where the sun moves, it keeps its face to the sun. That motion, that holy movement is *ska-ska,* the Sundance."

The chief lifts his head so the sun's full on his face. "Creator," he says. "Bless us here today. Have pity on us." His prayer is all about the four directions from whence we've come, about how the ones we've left behind and who've gone away from us are here now, in our hearts. His voice speaks to me of the rootedness we seek, called so many names by so many tongues. He prays long and hard and sincerely—you can tell he means it with every bit of heart he can muster. He prays for the dancers, for our mothers and for our children, for the plant nation who we must make relatives with or perish, for the animal nation that it might send messengers and lookouts, guidance and vision. He prays for the four-leggeds and the creepy craw-lies and the winged ones, that they might come and fly over the dancers, keep keen watch and keep us safe. He prays a prayer like I've never heard, long and loud so I look around and many are weeping outright, silver tears running down the men's cheeks onto bare chests, many of which bear the tell-tale scars of piercings. The bent arm becomes a pipe, *canupa wakan*, which gets held up as he prays his gratitude to White Buffalo Calf Woman, how she came down from the hills one day when the people were starving and had no medicine. Of the first two men who were sent to meet her, one lusted for her body and was turned to stone, that stone to dust, and the other's heart was good. He brought her among the people and she gave the holy gift of the pipe and taught how to use it. She walked away, and when she reached the hillside, the people watched her transform into a white buffalo calf. Buffalo appeared then and the plants brought forth all medicines and the people were healthy again. *Canupa wakan*, the pipe that White Buffalo Calf Woman brought with her own hands, is wrapped this second in a holy place, overlooked to this day by Chief Arvel Looking-horse, whose grandmother named him pipe carrier when he was a twelve-year-old boy—the last one forever, she said.

True Heart prays with the pipe, the smoke curling above his grey hair, mingling with the words and the wind and the spotted eagle wings that flash, fanning the smoke for all of us to breathe. The fire is burning better now, kept by a wiry Canadian named Sandy, who's head fireman.

Across from me, with the Utah people, Red Holy's wife yells for me to take off my hat, she mimes someone taking off a ballcap. True Heart, I notice, is wearing a ballcap, with Veteran printed above the bill.

The dancers are asked to fill their *canupas*. Fifty kneel on unfolded sheets of colored cloth and begin the slow work of praying over their tobacco which is really not tobacco at all, but *wichasha*, a mix of mullein, sage and willow bark and ingredients I haven't learned yet. A handful is held up to the sun and prayed over for a painfully long time. Then, carefully, the tobacco is tamped into the bowl of the pipe head, holy pipestone from the monument in Minnesota where the buffalo all lay down and died ancestral deaths, turned by spirit into the stone from which all pipestone is cut. The bowl symbolizes the female spirit, fitted into the male stem which is wrapped with sage and animal totem—I've seen ermine and rabbit ear, porcupine quill, mallard. Sixty dancers pray this way over tobacco, reach fistfuls to the sun.

Then, pipes filled, the dancers stand in the circle, True Heart at its center, and hold the pipestems to the sun. The man Florida Boy is here to support—a physician's assistant from Melbourne, Florida—he's weeping hard now, his *canupa* wavering. Beside me, a sixty-some-year-old couple each hold a *canupa* to the sky, praying loudly in unison. To my left is a beautiful Lakota woman, long black hair braided and hanging over a pure white dress; her three-year-old daughter helps her hold the pipe up to Grandfather, *Tunkasila*, the great mystery. Nicki is directly in front of me; she's placed the pipe bowl to her forehead, the male stem points to the same sun I've been seeing for my whole life, only different, not what sunflowers lean toward. I hear the words that come out of her mouth, and am very moved. I think of my wife and daughter, recall the lovely songs in Evangeline's lodge and how she introduced me to her own children as *Uncle*, someone for them to watch for I must die soon on that mountain, how there was great dignity in that, in crying for a vision unto death. I remember thinking how anybody that loved me would love the ceremony, and that's what I'm thinking now. With my heart's heart, I'm thinking that anyone who loves these people would love this ceremony. Then the lighting begins and I'm running for wooden matches.

"Do we have veterans here?" True Heart says, after the *canupas* are prayer smoked.

Fifteen men raise hands, including Charley, the milk-eyed flutist. They meet in a circle in the center of the circle, introduce themselves and tell their title, where they served. True Heart was in Korea; Charley—Vietnam. A big man named Hawk who walks humped over with a cane is Operation Desert Storm. The men weep openly during the introductions. My own tears are a surprise—all this craziness, the firekeeper within and without—I'm against the war, have marched my daughter in peace rallies where *patriots* sling insults and venom. Jill's father's a Navy Captain. During the January before Iraq and all that "shock and awe" bullshit, he visited and I got him down to the courthouse with Lyra for a peace rally. He was bossman on three different destroyers during Vietnam, wore a hat with Tin Can Sailors writ on it, and Channel 5, Salt Lake's Mormon television station, interviewed him. That night we sat in front of the tv and watched him speak out against wars of aggression, my four-year-old daughter dancing circles around him. All these vets come to the dance, True Heart hauls out an American flag, and the whole bunch of them walk the two hundred yards to the arena flagpole in silence. Across the distance, I see them praying as the flag is hoisted beside the Native American Flag. Men salute, move hands over their hearts. A song is sung. As if on prompt, *wanbli* circles above. Sometimes, not very often, but sometimes, you know a moment's import as it happens, how you'll hold onto it, replay it until a groove forms in your mind. The colorful flags whip in the wind, a sound like sheets ripping on a clothesline before an Arkansas thunderstorm. Like a sunflower—energy and motion.

When it's over, the Utah group meets at Red Holy's R.V. I sit cross-legged under tall pine, self-conscious. Red Bear's wife is here, Marie, a real serious looking dancer who's either very kind or mean as hell, or both, I can't tell. Beside me sits a badly wounded carpenter—he's recently mangled his hand in a table saw—who is here to support a dancer named Boar. Behind us, a heat and air guy with his fourteen-year-old daughter and son; his blonde wife has this scared look in her eye. She's trembling. Seventy-year-old Dean Red Cloud has driven here from New York City; he's Red Holy's brother in the Indian sense—really, they just ran into each other on a dirt road outside Albuquerque and both wore their hair the same way, burr cut on top and grown long down the back. There's Joe who rode his Harley Davidson here, and another couple whose bare-midriffed daughter never takes her eyes off the cell phone in her hands. Nicki and Mailman sit on lawn chairs with sun in their eyes. And there's Tara, a dark-haired beauty, she looks absolutely nothing in the world like somebody about to offer flesh.

Red Holy is dead serious, he lays out the rules, what goes and what doesn't. Absolutely no owl feathers. Anyone wearing eagle must be registered, which I take means Indian. Raven and hawk—no problem. No crossing the eastern gate which unites the dancers with the rising sun; cross the eastern gate and the dance is over. No pictures. No drugs or alcohol. No taking anything seriously. Thoughts are energy—*watch your thoughts*. Anyone gets in trouble, look at the tree. Tree'll take care of you.

I don't know what he does in life, Red Holy, but he claims to be one of the original inventors of crack cocaine, cooking it up way back before anybody else. He feels guilty, *responsible*, he says. Red Holy was hell on wheels, I have a feeling. He's maybe fifty, fifty-one. Out in the world, I'd buy him a beer. Have many a fine nipperkin.

Everybody has a chance to talk, always the hardest part for me to take, listening. The heat and air guy gifts Joe with a beat up eagle wing. Dean tells a story about how we'll remember nothing but good from all this. Tara could double for Mary Ann on Gilligan's Island, twin braids dyed jet black. I say I'm happy to support Nicki, that I hope I'll be able to do what I need to do. This is a compassionate dance. Unbelievable things are about to happen, Red says. He's dreamed this whole thing out, he's already lived it, it's part of his DNA.

7.

We are gathered at last year's tree, a forty-footer, wrapped head to toe in prayer ties, tobacco pinched into squares of colored cloth. Each dancer must tie a hundred-and-one of these in each of the sacred colors: black for west, red for north, yellow for east and white for south. One extra tie is added, so each dancer arrives at the tree with four-hundred-and-five ties. Work is prayer—twenty thousand ties for sixty dancers and, like the tree itself, they're not allowed to touch the ground. True Heart prays to the year-dead tree, he puts both hands on it, throws his face to the sky and prays in the strong voice. He thanks the Sundance tree, tells it what's to come, how we'll dig it up, smoke the holy *canupa* buried beneath it, then burn it for the purification lodge this evening.

Last year's dancers gather at the base. Shovels appear, bars and picks. A tremendous digging commences, the powder dust rising. It's noon, not a cloud in the blue sky. This is the sort of work I grew up on, shovel in hand, digging. The poet Seamus Heaney writes of digging, how it connects us to our ancestors and roots. The first few feet come up fast before we hit stone. One shovel sings out, so Charley waves his arms and everybody backs off. He crawls down into the hole and wrestles out a huge stone that's wedged against the tree trunk. Then there's another stone and another, and the digging turns into hard labor. Men take turns crawling down into the hole and doing the work with their hands. When the red-wrapped stem of the *canupa* is unearthed, Charley crawls in again and works for thirty minutes straight to get it out unharmed, which—I'll be damned—he does. The other dancers fall away in reverence. To me it's just a pipe that's been buried under a tree—these ceremonies have symbols built into symbols, that's how it seems.

After another hour's backbreaking work, all last year's dancers spread out in the circle. Feet planted on where they recollect being set free from the tree, they take bloodstained ropes and lean into the weight. The rest of us work the trunk, lower the tree down onto sawhorses, so no part touches the ground. Prayer ties are carefully stripped off, burned, and a man with foot-long braids chainsaws the tree foot to crown. He says, "Get outta my way. I work this mother like a Ginsu knife," and that's exactly what he does, working his Stihl clean as a chef's knife. Even here, there's a ceremonial way to cut up a Sundance tree, something about cutting the forks from the limbs only in certain numbers. Each piece is cut in a specific way for a specific reason and blankets are moved along so that not even the sawdust touches the ground. Sandy, boss fireman for this whole show, digs the fire pit into a perfect circle, enlarging it to six feet across. He lays down fifty-six stones for two purification lodges, one male, one female, and the first pieces of the Sundance tree burst afire. The *canupa* is prayed with by the four men I've come to recognize as Sundance Chiefs—TrueHeart, Roberto—a Lakota man from St. Louis who'll run things on the floor, Willy Day, a stone mason and pipe carrier I met in Salt Lake when building Nicki and Mailman's first *inipi*, and Hernando—an Incan who True Heart's adopted as a spiritual son. The four men smoke the unburied pipe and the air gets heavy, hard to breathe.

A little rain falls.

Then comes a sweet terrible downpour, like the sky roof's fallen.

All afternoon I work alongside the one-armed carpenter who's come with the Utah people to rebuild a spindly trailer we'll use to haul this year's tree from somewhere sixty miles out on Zuni Land. Everybody that can use tools has been summoned. The finished product is suspect at best, a flimsy frame built up over Boar's truck to hold the trunk, followed by a long trailer with a cradle that supports another thirty feet of tree. It's got to be illegal as hell, what we come up with for carrying the tree, that's what I'm thinking by afternoon, when it's clear and hot again and we reassemble for tree day. With our departure, maybe two-hundred jam into vehicles of every kind. Back on Great White Father Road as a quarter-mile entourage, we turn on headlights and flashers per state law for funeral processions, then converge on, and entirely destroy, the one combo gas station and convenience store. Mailman lets me borrow four bucks for Jumbo Scoop Fritos which I devour. We wait for Nicki to use the indoor plumbing before we're off again—across the desert, all us White Indians following Chief True and a pot-bellied Navajo named Leslie who knows where the cottonwood grows.

Monday afternoon, 5:00 p.m. lit up on Mailman's dashboard, I can't help seeing Jill, my good wife, back in Salt Lake with Lyra. Straight up happy hour, she's just poured a first glass of wine and retired to the back patio where shade has pooled near the garden. Crookneck squash is putting on a show though the tomatoes are slow this year, just now ripening. Lyra's kiddie pool is filled with the icy clear water that comes from Mountain Dell Reservoir—so cold that our roofer once passed clean out after drinking a mason jar full in the three o'clock sun. My daughter's wearing her blue one piece from last year, riding down the slide, splashing the pear and plum, the good tan showing from our river trip. Jill's reading, thinking about grilling chicken over charcoal with split squash on the side. She's past asking herself, "Who on earth am I married to? What's happened to him?" In Nicki's backseat, staring through tinted windows at Zuni Land, the heart of Indian country, the thought of my small family in our backyard on the edge of the Wasatch foothills breaks my heart—hurts me to the core. I feel irresponsible and stupid and gullible and downright negligent. A blowout or a flipped truck, what's to keep me from dying out here? What if my daughter has to grow up never knowing her father, just like I did? The pain in my side, the quaver in my hands these days, it's no joke. The rattlesnake unfurled real fangs, and that was real wind that chased my ass out of Butler Wash. And now, I'm very much here in god knows where New Mexico, in the backseat of a stuffy Four Runner, on my way with two-hundred some other oddballs to chop down a living cottonwood tree, give the son of a bitch a funeral and plant it in a hole to string people up on with very real stobs skewered through their flesh. Very real, *no shit.* In the front seat, Nicki and Mailman are talking about missing turns, about the history of the turns they've missed while driving. From the pocket of my shorts, I fish what I least expect: "Daddy, I love you," the short note says. Lyra's drawn herself as the star princess. Her words sear.

I see it shining way off in the distance.

Three miles north and east of where we drive, a green seam coils against a redrock cliff ridge. In the desert west, you learn to spot water at a distance, to recognize the signs. I think, what beautiful trees, when the long entourage in front of us busts off the two-lane onto a gravel road and a mighty dust cloud rises in the windless sky, and still the cottonwoods—I can't tell how many from here—shine, that creamy white on their trunks that painters exaggerate. Our dust flies straight up and hangs. The trees get nearer, three I can tell. By the time we reach the field, fifty vehicles are already parked. Men, women and children—many little girls dressed in swirling skirts—stream across dried up rows of corn toward the only three trees visible in any direction as far as the eye can see.

Beyond the field's back edge, green grass grows down a slope to a wash where water must have flowed not so long ago. After six now, the three silvery trees throw long shadows over the green grass, the gentle slope and hollow where we gather. All together now for the first time, I get a picture of who we are—the dancers are mostly all here, bare-chested men with farmer tans and women in braids. They've grown their hair out and most are between thirty and fifty. Soft bellies and many of them can't use tools, which says middle class, bank accounts, campers and RVs, travel, flush for the extravagance of ceremony. These aren't poor folk, they have chainsaws and good knives and drive brand new extra heavy-duty Chevrolets. The women are pretty and white, mostly, granola girls with bright dresses and shampooed braids. One is a dead ringer for Gwyneth Paltrow, a woman whose beauty freezes. Her blonde hair is meticulously combed—its shine blinds. Her skin is flawless pink, lotioned, not used to the sun. She looks never to have worked a day outside. Her cuticles are perfect, white half-moons show through each nail. I can't picture this woman starving, dehydrated, offering flesh.

One thing I've noticed about White Indians and ceremony, especially if real Indians have anything to do with the show, a lot of money gets passed around. Say five hundred dollars a pop, I've heard, to dance. My own *hanbleceya* cost over four hundred, by the time I got out of it, and I've heard of people charging five hundred dollars for a sweat lodge. At five hundred a piece times sixty dancers, that's thirty thousand dollars, most of which, I imagine, goes to the spiritual intercessor. Money is energy, that's how it gets explained. Though imagining the dancers, about to collectively donate a pound of human flesh, kicking in thirty grand to boot, that's beyond me, energy or no.

We congregate in the hollow where an earnest prayer is made for the tree. Chief holds hands up into the pinkening sky and thanks the tree for its life. And it is very much like a funeral, how True Heart talks about the tree people, what it's like to lose one of their own, and how much we are indebted for that life. Charley shimmies up the trunk, makes the lowest limbs—twenty feet off the ground—in seconds. I've seen enough of him now not to be surprised; he's in the treetop tying ropes, tossing down the loose ends. Then the youngest virgin—a little Indian girl whose mama is one of this year's dancers—is led to the base of the tree and handed a hatchet with a gleaming gold chopping blade. She's two-years-old, three at most, wearing an elaborately beaded dress that's been handmade for this moment. She issues the first chop, the initial wound into the silver flesh of the cottonwood that is now forevermore a Sundance tree.

A line is formed behind the youngest virgin; a four-year-old girl, a six-year-old, all the virgins on the ground have a turn at the tree—the lone chops echoing against the sandstone bluff. The older girls chop three, four times, with gusto and wide grins, actually start to do a little damage. One dressed in turquoise steps shyly to the tree where she is handed a full-fledged double-blade ax. Her first swing flat-blades the tree trunk. The second cuts flesh, and when she swings a third time, white tree meat flies shining above her head. Young boys are followed by the older boys who, in turn, are followed by the male Sundancers, youngest to oldest. By now, everyone who's not chopping has hold of a rope up above on the slope, the idea being that we lower the tree down into the hollow where it will be caught up by the congregation there, so that no part of the Sundance tree ever touches the ground, not ever. The youngest dancers chop as if their lives depend on it. They've never used axes before, some of them, and their swings are mostly just piss and vinegar, sheer bluster. The older dancers make headway. True Heart takes a swing, but it's Charley and Willy Day who sever the core. And I've got to tell you that this is one heavy-ass tree, it hauls thirty men with their ropes down in a fingersnap. I'm still not sure how in hell the men and women below manage to break its fall, or how on earth we manage to get it onto the trailer or out onto the highway or to the Sundance grounds. Time blurs. Once the tree falls, everything shifts gears, as if some terrible power has harnessed us to do its bidding.

8.

Only two things you can give to spirit—Evangeline says—time or flesh. She said it in lodge, laying against the eastern wall, where the flap had just been opened and sweet-cool January air was pouring in, driving away the heat that I'd believed would kill me a few minutes before. Sometimes the fear comes on you and your heart goes crazy and you dig your face up against the floor blanket that separates you from outside. Breathing gets to be a real problem. It's possible, if a merciful person has tied the lodge blankets, to burrow a few fingers out to form a crack, sip breathable air between your lips. I've witnessed grown men and women scream *mitakuye oyasin*, the signal for the door flap to be opened, crawl out and collapse on the earth, sometimes screaming in pain. And I've heard water pourers refuse to open doors. Sometimes somebody says something that makes the air unbelievably heavy—like the night when I was fireman and a face I couldn't see began talking about his brother who'd just died, the heft of sorrow and guilt he felt. My own brother died in a one-car crash when he was nineteen, out drinking and driving on a country road in Arkansas, the shortcut I'd taught him home from the college in Conway. So this guy in lodge started talking about his dead brother. I was fireman, responsible for bringing in the rocks, the water and cedar and *canupa*, opening and shutting the door flap. At first, I went to my hands and knees, then full on the ground. I dug through the bottom flap but none of the outside air would come to me and my heart got beating and I honestly thought I would suffocate right then in there, listening to the story of the guilt this brother felt for his dead brother. After I was outside, heaving by the fire pit, I wondered how I'd ever get back in: who opens the door for the one who opens the door? This all comes to me out of nowhere, the green cottonwood boughs bouncing this way and that, the silver flesh shining on the cradle beneath turquoise sky.

Getting the tree to Cougar's ranch and the Sundance grounds is one hell of a feat. For one thing, the road up to the ranch is narrow with tight turns punctuated by big pines that stop us again and again. Still, many have made it back to camp and we can hear the drumbeats there, how they ready for our arrival, which gives us energy and will. I feel entirely part of this now, as if it's what I'm supposed to be doing, walking on foot beside the tree, pushing and heaving when need be. It matters. With maybe thirty minutes of light left, we arrive, and what I can only describe as the sound of jubilation goes up against the sunset, and it feels like we've brought some great and long-awaited gift to the people. We carry the tree on our shoulders outside the length of the arena, through the eastern gate. We haul it in and lay her on sawhorses set every ten feet up to the hole which is man-deep now, immaculately cleaned. A loud silence comes over us and True Heart raises his hands, the prayer rolling off his lips to the four directions and the sky and the earth and the inside of all things. This close to sunset, shafts of light zigzag across the sky in an arc that makes a huge semi-circle around us. A *winkte* notices—I see him trace the sky marks with his finger tip.

A horde of dancers descend on the tree; head to foot, it's maybe sixty feet tall, and every scrap of space is taken by people unrolling colorful bundles of prayer ties that get wrapped in clockwise circles. A *winkte* ties on the effigy of a muscular man with an enormous penis. A yard timber gets tied across the uppermost limbs like the cross section of a crucifix, a point that doesn't yet register with me but will. I help Nicki unroll her prayer ties, one hundred and four each of black, red, yellow and white, then one color of her choosing. When I asked her why she's dancing, she said that her people, the ones that have passed away, cry out for her, that they're haunted and fill her dreams for reasons I won't mention save to say the spirits see patterns repeating in real life.

After the twenty-thousand plus prayer ties come the ropes, each one with its own halter—two straps with loops to secure the skewers. The dancers lace ropes into knots, unfurl the lengths to the halters, each one bearing tufts of cloth meant to cover the piercings, if only for a moment, before flesh snaps. This is solemn work, the tying on of so many prayers, and the weight of what's coming sinks in some. We form a circle, put our shoulders into the tree, lift it high enough so the ones with ropes begin to pull. I see no way in hell of raising the tree, but huge skeins of fabric get the wind, begin to whip, and it rises, the dancers hauling with the ropes and us pushing from the bottom until, finally, the trunk thuds, seeds. The inverse of the initial digging takes place; big rocks are levered down to hold the tree, everyone that came out goes back in, and the *canupa*, filled with *wichasha* and wrapped tightly in a green garbage bag is placed facing north. Charley covers it gently with dirt from his hands. Then, just as dark comes, with the lodge fire bright where last year's tree burns, we rake the last clods out, feathering fill dirt against the trunk. The slick-barked cottonwood might have grown here all along. Dark with prayer ties and sap now, the heat of the day is still on it, that sunshine smell of grasshoppers whirring and afternoons that last till midnight.

We form a circle around the tree, around the breadth and depth of the Sundance ground. Look at the tree, how the last light brushes the topmost leaves, the small man with the enormous penis up there waving. Packs of wild wolves are stirring from sleep, a full moon casting bloody shine on broken bottle shards across the fat bellied world. For the third time this day, True Heart prays out loud. My stomach's growling and I'm a hundred miles of thirst, lord god how an iced beer would go down now. Three hundred yards west, the white kitchen tent shines. I grew up hungry, it's a feeling I understand in my core; sometimes I'll get out of bed, walk to the refrigerator in the dark, make a peanut butter and jelly sandwich and wash it down with cold milk. And I remember my own mother feeling her way up the halls of my childhood, the eerie light thrown from the refrigerator while she rummaged for something to eat. Buffalo stew tonight, that's the word, the last supper before the dancer's four day fast. I imagine the stew simmering up on gas fires under the kitchen tents, the potatoes and carrots, onion and celery, Florida Boy stirring the savory soup with a boat paddle.

A man I recognize as a Utah dancer appears dead center of the circle. Just like that he throws his head back and lets fly the four directions song, loud enough for the wolves to hear ten miles off. He faces each direction with the song, then his voice blows out, goes ragged. The whole lot of us limp uphill in the dark, up to the soup line where bowls are ladled. I carry mine to bed, eat and steal a nap before purification.

Who can say what time it is when I wake up looking through the tent's star window, the faint light falling on a picture of my daughter? Jill's here too—the three of us listening to wolves, one individual's voice bleeding into another and another. Head blood from the summer gash stains the tent wall, dark remnants. I pull on clean shorts, zip the tent door behind me. Outside, the air is good and chill. The ant people munch watermelon rinds in the blackness of earth tunnels. Stars are delirious over my head and all down the hill I can see sparks whirling.

Rocks for the sweat lodge glow red hot. Last year's tree has given its ghost heat—the flesh that has twisted in the wind from its limbs all the days of the year. The baby bundle hung there on Easter, it presided over this earth when the grass grew green, when the red-headed hummers flew up from South America, when the ant people built their mounds and the snake nation shed skin. Now is purification—tonight we wander down the hill, dragging moonshadow behind every footfall.

I join Red Holy and all the towel-draped Sundancers in a line outside the male lodge. Roberto, the tall Lakota who the lawn and garden salesman followed here from St. Louis, will pour water. The women stretch in an equal line on the other side of the fire pit. The light dances through the women's dresses, outlines thighs. Their voices are sweet melodies, their laughter ringing. They disappear into the mouth of the lodge and I hear their drums quicken, the voices launching into song.

A Kiowa boy who's traveled here with a lame Indian named Hawk is fireman—carrying in the women's twenty-eight stones two at a time. With the men, there's some sort of hierarchy—Red Holy's saying something about it, maybe oldest first—his brother's here from New York, seventy-five years old with a long greying ponytail. Inside, Roberto sprinkles the hot rocks with cedar. The door comes down and I'm in the dark with thirty some men, some I know and some I don't. The first round begins when Roberto tells us what we need to know, how it is to be here alive at this moment. We're instructed on what to expect for tomorrow's dance and this wonderful singer from Mexico sings three songs as beautiful as I've ever heard. A lone wolf howls. The heat is intense. I hear the women's voices through the lodge walls. I think of home. I try to sing from my heart, to mean this. People are breathing. The labored breaths are silenced by the hiss of water on lightning-hot stone.

9.

Before light on Sundance morning, July 19, 2005, the dancers sweat two rounds, fourteen stones, into the spirit world. Fireside, there's much whispering. Nervous laughter as *canupas* are filled. The woman who looks like Gwyneth Paltrow has combed honey-blonde hair out to its full shining length. Her white dress is punctuated by a medicine amulet with spokes of many colors. Seen in the flash of firelight she is heartbreak beautiful. Tara, a Utah dancer, picks me out of the dark. "You're here," she says. Last night, walking back from purification, she'd said out of the clear blue, "I can tell you're compassionate. You care deeply about people." I don't know where that came from, why she said it to me. True Heart's here, his hair falling to a ceremonial shirt—black, yellow, red and white embroidery down the neck's V and the cuffs of the sleeves.

The men wear red skirts, waist to ankle. A fresh woven sage hoop crowns each head, criss-crossed just above their eyes so the hoop's open horn protrudes on the forehead above each eye. Sage wristbands and anklets are tied similarly, the loops crisscross and make horns. Barechested, a medicine wheel medallion hangs between their nipples. All save Charley's feet are moccasined and they all carry pipes, freshly filled and prayed over. Many fan hawk wings, the light-colored trailing sides flashing. A *winkte* flaps his raven. The tall Lakota, Willy Day, has feathers from *Wanbli Gleska*, whose spotted plumes are the most holy save the pure white that flutter from the butt of Brave Heart's staff. Roberto from St. Louis carries eagle's wings and a staff decorated with *wamblechi.* With the stars overhead and the fire and the last wolves singing out for the night, these thirty male dancers, some praying, some dancing already, humming the song, they make a sight—much energy here, the sparks roiling.

Light comes. The drums strike up from the south side of the dance grounds. A song begins, a striking melody that is calm and peaceful and res-olute. These words seem new, to have been born this second from the head singer's mouth, whose voice is hoarse and powerful. *Tunkasila,* he sings, *pilamaya yelo hey.* The old words soar and fall, the drum thump-thumping. Dancers line the northern wall, women then men joined by *winktes,* Red Wolf, a dancer named Balance with his raven wing, and the southern wom-an-man who brought me eggs when I was fireman. He's from Tennessee hill country, not far from Knoxville, joined by a Ph.D. in mathematics from University of Oregon.

Earlier, True Heart beckoned me. Just after first light he motioned for me to come. He looked me in the eye, waved a hand. He'd seen through. Next second he'd ask me to dance and I'd die on that tree—what am I so afraid of in this life? My heart banged. It wasn't fear—not exactly. More like what happens to you in a deer stand when a six point buck walks into the clearing and you raise the gun and take aim, and your heart goes apeshit. *Buck Fever* hunters call it. Pure adrenalin rushes through your veins, fear purified to its most powerful part. What my ancestor hunter needed in the moment of the kill, wild energy flowing. But I wasn't asked to dance. Instead, I was handed a bundle of willow stakes—twenty-eight of each color. Wrapped with red, yellow, white and black cloth, they make the inner-circle. "Put them up," he said. "Cut a sapling for flesh offerings. Place it at the northern gate." And even though I've never been here before, that's what I did, put them up—twenty-eight in each of the four quadrants. The Kiowa boy helped. I learned the right distance, used a digging iron to make the holes, while the Kiowa boy sifted *winchasha* into each, stomping stakes into the holes. Together we crafted a perimeter.

Firemen carry metal cans of hot coals, sprinkling in handfuls of cedar from shoulder bags. Smoke billows on either side of the dancers as Willy Day and Hernando fan *azilia* with eagle's wings. The line of dancers is complete now—women first, then men. True Heart's in front, followed by red-skirted Roberto and Willy Day. Chief's staff shines with white eagle feathers, the holiest. They prepare to make the procession to the eastern gate, to enter the Sundance ground with the rising sun. Sunlight splashes the tree now, shining on the highest leaves. The holy men move to the head of the line: Roberto takes the lead, he'll direct the Sundance from the inside, from the spirit world. His braid is undone, grey strands running down his red back. His hands make quick directions. True Heart follows, in long pants and the ceremonial shirt. He too, I see, wears spotted *wanbli* feathers in his hair. Behind is Hernando, the Incan man he'd adopted in a *kiva* ceremony two nights ago. Hernando is thirty, maybe thirty-five; he wears the red skirt, moccasins and medicine wheel amulet. Then Willy Day and all the women dancers.

The sight of the women shocks. Oldest to youngest, thirty of them in shining handsewn dresses. The colors bleed brightly from one to the next. Nicki is near the front. Grey-headed, she wears the sage crown, wristlets and anklets. The singers kick in with the big kettle drum on the circle's south side. In full pageantry, the line parades around the northern wall. The dancers walk erect—either the bravest people I've ever seen, or downright crazy. Maybe they're on fire with fear, like I'd be. Or they somehow repress the fact that they're about go without food or water for four days, not to mention having hunks of flesh carved off, all the while dancing on ground so hot that it burns straight through the best mocassin leather. Maybe it's a beautiful moment for them, just outside the eastern gate. They are immaculate, all of New Mexico seeming to fall away behind them where the sun's gold curve now shows. Here is the moment—energy in motion. Behind the Sundance Chief, in full regalia, they halt for a moment, then enter with the full risen sun.

Sundance ground is a perfect circle, forty yards or so in diameter, with a circumference that is everywhere equidistant from the tree. Dancer is to tree as earth is to sun, imitating the clockwise revolutions of the terrestrial sphere. Inside the circle is a slightly smaller circle, formed by one hundred twelve willow stakes—twenty-eight each of yellow, white, black and red—which divide the dance arena into quadrants of east, west, north and south. The ring's apex is the eastern gate, where the sun and the dancers enter each of the four mornings of Sundance. A forbidden zone, no one is allowed to break the eastern gate's plane; to walk past the opening is to bring an immediate end to the dance. Standing in the eastern gate, looking west, one stares straight into the prayer-wrapped cottonwood to the western gate—the circle's nadir—which passes straight through the center of the firepit, beyond which, on either side, is an *inipi*. In this way, an open path is maintained between fire, tree and sun. Standing just behind the firepit, one can see through the whole thing: outside to inside to outside.

A flesh offering tree—for supporters and guests—is embedded at the circle's northern gate, beyond which is the Moon Shed, built for any menstruating female. Should a woman dancer enter her moon, a supporter immediately takes her place while she looks on in separation. Strong earth medicine, a woman on her moon, that's what I'm told. Go there often with cedar.

The southern gate is covered by an arbor that stretches all along the circle's hemisphere—from western gate to just shy of the eastern gate where a rope is tied to block passage. Outside this, a huge kettle drum is set up on a wooden stand where prayer songs are sung under the arbor's tolerable shade. Guests and supporters dance in place, left foot, right foot, left foot— the singing constant. During the trying moments when piercings fail to rip loose, some cry out for the blood of their loved ones under the arbor in the long curve from west to forbidden eastern gate.

The living theater of Sundance is a spectacle beyond belief, a *circulous vitiosus* where beauty and horror intermingle freely. The circus is replete with clowns and demons—the backward-forward *heyokas* who speak directly to the audience; they cajole the crowd especially during the goriest moments of spectacle, thus serving exactly as the chorus does in a Greek tragedy. Across the Sundance stage march primary and secondary actors in their costumes. Of the spirit world, they can neither speak nor be spoken to. Their faces are masks, the husk eyes simultaneously gazing on life and death. The conflicts that play out during the days without food and water, produced and directed and choreographed by the intercessor and his stage hands, are profound. *Deus ex Machina* appear in the forms of the bull bison head worn by the lead dancer—in this case the potbellied Navajo named Leslie who promptly gores a *winkte's* ass. Each male dancer wears a bone whistle made from eagle's wing, which he blows in times of need, so that nearly thirty men dance shrill whistling as a song grows loud and a fellow dancer offers up pieces of himself to the great sun father. On the second day of the dance, buffalo skulls are lined up inside the eastern gates. Meat covers the skulls, they've never been boiled or bleached, and so must be heavily *aziliaed* with sage and cedar, before the ropes are tied to the horns then laced through the sharp-pointed pegs that pierce the men's shoulders. A dancer drags as many skulls as it takes, round and round the circle till the flesh breaks free. And if it doesn't, if for some reason the man's skin won't turn loose, the chorus of *winkte's* and *heyokas* will work the crowd, burn cedar to break the tension, because it can be a horrible thing to look on. Women make the piercing *yee-yee-yee-yee-yee* call in their throats and the resulting catharsis is very real and touching.

Guests and supporters stream down into the southwest gate. Sandy gives me a fire can wired to a forked willow stick, along with a shoulder bag of cedar that he says to go easy on, we don't want too much smoke. Me and a guy named Kirk are responsible for smudging off everyone entering, some two hundred who drift under the arbor shade which is a relief from the increasingly fierce heat. Roberto leads the dancers into a V that spreads across the arena's northern quarter. The women V directly inside the men, stepping meticulously, the sun full on their faces, and the old Sundance song takes shape on their bright lips. The ever-widening V's are formed moving south to west to north, a clockwise mirror of Earth's year-long revolution around it's pole star, and the apparent motion of the sun. Each dancer carries a pipe. Roberto gives the sign and the dancers reach their pipes into the sky, hold the female *canupa* bowls to their hearts and stretch the wooden stems to the sun. Finally, all directions done save east where the sun hangs still, each dancer leans the pipe against a rail that's been built near the western gate.

Drumbeat and song cease. Roberto leads the dancers into a human circle—the men and women I've come to recognize span the entirety of the Sundance globe. They stand at full attention, their collective nerves electric. They look at the tree. *Tree will take care of you—in trouble, look at the tree*, Red Holy said. A silence falls over us. Sandy, head fireman, carries a bundle out to the tree. He unrolls a buffalo robe at its base. A medical waste cannister is opened: latex gloves, gauze, a razorblade—I don't know what all—are taken out. Willy Day leads a tall tattooed man with a black ponytail around the perimeter; he tugs the man's sage wristlet. They pass my smudge bucket, sweet cedar smoke rising, then in front of each of the dancers whose eyes have grown wide and white these last moments. Day before yesterday, this same man helped me set teepees for the dancers, telling how his son had only last week been shot in the head during a convenience store robbery. This man, he'd just come from spreading his dead son's ashes. Jesus, I thought, there's a story that'll walk right up and kick your ass.

Willy Day leads the man by his sage wristband, each foot lifting in the slight dance. The tattooed man raises both arms high above his head, leaning back into the tree so his broad chest shines colorfully. The *Tunkasila* song begins and the drum heartthrums. Under the arbor, hundreds are singing, lifting hands to the treetop for each *Tunkasila*. *Thank you for giving us this to do*—the song means. Hernando raises an arm. The razor blade flashes. He cuts a piece of flesh from each side of the man's chest, just above the nipples. The blood runs down suddenly, without warning. Later, I'll learn that this is the flesh offering that begins the dance. Most often, an elder is chosen, but the man whose son had been killed was adamant. For now, the shock worms its way into my guts. And I can tell by the faces under the arbor that I'm not the only one. The sweet music washes over us and this sacrificed man drips a trail of very real blood all around the arena. When he's out of the circle and under the arbor again, I watch him raise his hands and join the *Tunkasila—thank you for giving us this to do.* Blood runs under his armpits, down his back and belly, sluicing over the panther and eagle and holy ghost tattoos, dripping into the dirt at his feet.

10.

A woman dressed in a purple kimono enters the westernmost part of the arbor where there's good deep shade for the dancers' rest between rounds. Her black hair twists into a tight bun held by wooden hairpins. She moves in measured steps, inspecting every inch under the arbor, picking up and straightening, arranging each chair. She's Shinto, a priestess, I'll learn, here to work energy. Shintos worship the deities of nature, they claim kinship to the sun goddess. Until we dropped nuclear bombs on top of their heads, Shinto was the state religion of Japan. Her face is immaculately made. I watch her from the fire pit. Our eyes meet. A white-gloved hand beckons. I enter the west gate. In the arena, the dancers are going through an elaborate pipe giveaway ceremony; each dancer's supporter lines up on the southern perimeter and accepts the choreographed gift. True Heart's out there, Roberto, Hernando. Nicki's grey hair shines.

"What is your name," the woman asks. She worries each word. Her eyes are deep brown. She's older than I thought, sixty maybe, serene as polished stone. She repeats my name twice, a good sound.

I nod. "What about you?"

She says, "Koo Wan."

During the Tree Ceremony, when the prayer ties were being wrapped, there was a Japanese girl with a hawk's wing and prayer tie bundle, accompanied by a husband. Though I haven't seen her among the dancers, these two women are relatives.

We shake hands.

"Can you bring a piece of wood," Koo Wan asks. "For his foot," she says and grimaces, so I know it's hurting him and she feels the pain plenty deeply.

She holds her hands three feet apart, and I retrieve a log chunk and set it end up as a footrest. "Thank you," she says and arranges then rearranges it in front of the chair where the Sundance Chief will sit. Then she takes a seat directly behind where his back will be, folds her hands into her lap and bows her head. She loves him, True Heart. "For his foot," Koo-Wan had said, wrapped in silk, a strong, strange woman.

The first piercings take place before the real heat comes. Once again Sandy carries the buffalo robe out on his shoulder, unrolls it at tree's base. A man is led around the circle by his wristlet—Sundancers are holy, the living must not touch them. He lay down on the buffalo robe. The sage crown is taken off his head and stuffed into his mouth, between his teeth. Hernando stretches on the latex gloves, strips a scalpel from plastic wrapper and makes the slices on either side of the man's chest. When skewers are forced through the slits of skin, toes curl. Muted screams gurgle in throats. Hernando doesn't like this. Carrying *azilia*, I'm seeing him intensely, and I don't think he likes the cutting. The pierced man is laced into a halter, a V-shaped piece of rope that connects to the sharpened piercing stobs above each nipple. A snatch of red cloth is arranged to fit against each pierce so onlookers cannot see the wounds outright. He takes his place at the nine o'clock position, puts his weight into the rope so it tightens and his chest flesh stretches like pink taffy. Another man lies down on the buffalo robe, then walks to three o'clock, leans his weight into the rope. A piercing song accompanies the drumbeat. Seeing this, it's like when somebody's real sick, about to die, and you know that they're going to die, only there's no getting ready, and when they quit breathing air it knocks you for a loop. *Wakan tanka, tunka-sila!* the people sing.

A woman is led to the buffalo robe. This Navajo head dancer, his chest is scar on top of scar. "Get in here," he says. Head dancer motions me inside the circle. He tells me to *azilia* the supporters who'll stand behind their dancer to catch them when they break free of this earth. The ceremony is elaborate, how each Sundancer is allowed many supporters; behind his back they sob, sing, lift and lower feet.

For the first time I notice the circles that are drawn on the men's chests, marking the spots where the piercings are to take place. The size of a silver dollar, the red circles are drawn with a fingertip dripped in ground pipestone. Some are egg-shaped—some stare like hollow eyes. They chill me, how one must tell another, *draw here*.

Hernando pierces the thickest part of the woman's biceps. Something goes wrong. Fear flashes across his eyes. Most have an eagle feather skewed through and go without being tethered to the tree. If a woman's given birth, all debts are paid and piercing is an insult to spirit. But here's this woman on the buffalo robe. She's got a dazed smile on her lips—like somebody fresh from a car wreck—big shiny eyes. When she backs up dead west, pulling the ropes tight, one of the skewers pops free, so the halter hooked to her other forearm flounces this way and that. Only this woman never even flinches. Again, she's walked to the buffalo hide. True Heart struggles out of his chair and walks out, slides on the rubber gloves and scalpels deeper piercings. Once again the woman backs up and lets her weight against the rope. I fan smudge and the song amplifies. An eagle circles above us, or a vulture—it's hard to tell. The dancers lean their full weight into ropes. It's a painful thing to see, horrible, though often described as beautiful. The actors tied to the tree of life, trying their flesh while clowns spin in all four directions—pure farce, pure tragedy. The circle is everywhere the same distance from the tree. Smudgers are dispatched with cedar, *pejuta* for the audience. From under the arbor, scores look on dumbstruck. Some sob. For many—like me—who've never witnessed such mutilation, the moment is simply beyond belief. When her piercings pop, the woman's led joyously around the dance arena, bright blood leaking down her forearms from the open wounds. Then the man at three o'clock—he's free, the sound like bullwhips cracking. But the last one, the man who's chosen nine o'clock, his piercings refuse to give. His chest flesh is elastic, it stretches a good half-foot, yaws tight then holds.

"*Hoka Ye!*" True Heart screams, and the man is brought back to the tree, which he touches with trembling fingertips. He cries. I recognize him as the physician's assistant from Melbourne, Florida, the one Florida Boy's here to support. I helped him move his tent from near the kitchen down to the dancer's tent sites. He talked about his wife, how this was hard for her, coming here from Florida, the heat, the dance. He needed to keep her comfortable, that's why we moved the tent, a cabin unit with two vestibules and a blow up mattress inside. True Heart makes the sign and the man begins to run backwards. I can see him straight in the face and the moment flattens out, hangs still for a few seconds. His eyes are wide, his nostrils flare. Crazy-eyed so you see why executioners cover the faces of the damned. He reaches full-speed. Rope snaps tight against halter. We all hear it—the sound. Tree's highest limbs tremble.

Winkte flaps raven wings; the one who's introduced himself to me as Balance is indeed balanced. He teaches dance at Temple University in Philadelphia, a place with a good writing program and every kind of person in the world living in the city. Who in hell are these people, us? Roberto initiates the pageantry that closes this first round—the V's form again, energy in motion. Willy Day fans cedar smoke from a bucket I hold knee-high. Dancers file through the western gate. They walk heavy, wipe sweat from their eyes. Some have let their sage crowns fall down over their eyes to block the sun and many have sunburned already. They sigh, take chairs, fall on their backs under the cool of the arbor shade. I walk out the western gate, around the firepit and find my water bottle. In the shade of the fire lodge, I roll and smoke one cigarette and then another. My hands shake. The smoke is comforting, takes the edge off. And though hot, the last of my spring water is good.

Midway through the second round, the operating theater is fully operational, one piercing then another and another—again and again and again the buffalo robe is spread out beneath the tree. Big puffs of cedar smoke are rising and Sandy has warned us that we're using too much, eyes are burning, stomachs turning. An Indian woman prays intensely. Kneeling, this woman talks to the base of the tree, her lips are moving. She's dark and lean and Hernando pierces her forearms and feathers—turkey, hawk, eagle maybe—are inserted through the slits. After, she's joyous. Her little black-haired daughter joins her and together they dance round the fairy ring and the heat comes on and the *winktes* make backward swirls in their turquoise skirts. I'm sent to *azilia* the moon shed where three woman watch from blankets. They smile, thank me. I feel nothing of their powerful connection to the earth, how their bleeding makes them conduits that somehow grounds spirit. The dancers' hand-dug toilet is ripe from here, a little breeze blowing in from the west. I'm dizzy. Every thought of Lyra and Jill goes through me like a spear.

The lawn and garden salesman's burned off his eyelashes. Tending a fire in hot daylight, it's hard to tell how close to get. He shovels coals into our buckets for smudge. People are coming and going on the path that's been set out along the dance ground's southern side. I've been told to keep an eye out, smudge all comers with the sweet cedar, and that's what I do, though I must tell you that it feels silly, how they raise arms and look at me with that unsure look, as if I know shit from shinola. The Tennessee *winkte* joins me. He has an unusual face, big with a broad forehead, so you'd expect this deep, resonant voice to come out of his mouth. "How y'all doin'?" he says.

I say, "Fine." A lie.

"Yonder comes a holy man."

A broad-shouldered white man with dingy blonde hair strides toward us like he knows what he's about, right past the firepit and the *inipis*. I dump a handful of cedar shake into my bucket, offer it when he passes. He doesn't look at me, but holds out two palms while he walks by, brings it to his chest. Next thing I know he's back, entering again, only this time he's wearing a black skirt and a buffalo hat, two horns standing up. This dead-serious look on his sixty-year-old face. He slides the buffalo hat, *Issiwun*, it's called, down over his brow, snorts, and charges the *winktes*. He gores Balance in the ass, grabs his own dick with one hand, scrotum with the other. "You ain't *heyoka*," he bawls, "if you don't go both ways." People in the crowd laugh, and before long he has us in the palm of his hand, following every move. A total surprise, this *heyoka*, how he arrives with the heat of the day and chases the Jesus out of the other clowns, right when things are getting serious, the piercings blending into one long operation punctuated by the bullwhip crack that skin makes when the skewers rip free. Anytime the *Tunkasila* song is sung, *heyoka* gets this wicked grin on his face, sticks an index finger in the air and spins. His chest and back are tattooed to mark the spots for piercings performed so many times that the ink has nearly vanished, long rows of scars from flesh offerings up and down either arm. And his neck has been slit, one tremendous scar above his Adam's apple, covering half his throat. He carries this whip, bits of bone and metal tied onto leather thongs, held by a loop around his wrist. I won't forget the whip. He trots against the clockwise flow, beats the Jesus out of the Tennessee *winkte*, then brings blood to his own thighs, grinning, stropping himself from one end of the sacred space to the other.

Before the second round's over, a big Indian shovels hot stones into the men's sweat lodge, carries in a bucket of water and sweats himself. I watch him from a distance, from inside the west arbor. I remember him joking with the dancers yesterday after the pipe loading ceremony. "Make sure and put on your sunscreen," he said. "Breakfast in the morning, powdered eggs, visionary, of course." And when we'd finished building the cradle for the tree, he'd inspected. "Boys, while I'm especially impressed that you've chosen galvanized nails for code purposes," he said, "I'll have to cite you for your lack of treated lumber."

We'd laughed. Here was Indian humor—the sort I'd read the spring before when my students plowed through Barry Lopez and Sherman Alexie. Now this man sweats himself in the lodge.

Steam pours from the *inipi* door when he crawls out on hands and knees, dresses. I watch him carry a medical waste canister to the northern gate, not twenty yards from the Moon shed. He sets up shop beside the sapling I put up this morning. Cedar wafts from the shade, fanned by *wambli gleska*. Soon a line will form. Sitting Bull, I will learn, before it was all over for him and his own stabbed him in the back, once had a hundred pieces of flesh cut from each arm during Sundance.

True Heart's words: *cut a fresh sapling for flesh offerings. Place it at the northern gate.*

11.

Hauling ass at 186,000 miles-per-second, sunlight blasts through ninety million miles in eight minutes. It roars over space and then, by the heat of day, knocks the Jesus out of us, waylays us, this godawful slap in the face. Indian time is now time—taste, sound, touch, smell, vision. All is warped under the kick-ass sun.

Three dancers go down.

Under the ferocious sun: one, two, three—they fall as deadweights.

An energy hurdles the arena's circumference.

To say that it is an *energy* is to say nothing of use; call it a fireball, a freight train, a goddamned *tsunami* of pure power plowing at the speed of light. I'm dumbstruck. Standing at the western gate, holding a smudge bucket, I'm dumbstruck. Over there a man has taken flesh offerings. The tree's tall as a five-story building. Three are down inside a second, my mind's just fast enough to see a second broken into parts, and each of the dancers falling in a part of that second. The energy moves clockwise. I'm seeing this with my eyes. A vision of profound violence seen through thick glass. Drums, voices, dream-vision, these all collide here and now.

The physician's assistant, bloody holes, an Oedipal eye above each nipple, reacts. Before I can even put the bucket down he's helping carry a dark-headed woman to arbor shade. Two more men lift the second one and, in this split second, I see the third, her silver hair shining.

Nicki. She looks for all the world like she's dead. Her head hangs at the end of her neck as she's carried through the west gate, straight past me. In my heart's heart, I know that Nicki is dead. They lay her limp body in the grass under a wedge of shade.

I'm floored.

The round ends suddenly. True Heart screams *Hoka Ye, medicine*. A man who's just returned from sightseeing drives his car to the to the main gate, says his air-conditioner's on high. I remember how Mama once hit the floor after viewing my brother, Steve, in his casket. The sound of her skull on a floor tile. And I recall the fearsome happy moment when I saw the quarter-size patch of brown, my daughter's hair, materialize from my wife's womb. And certain mornings when the sun is still far from rising, but the light faintly shows through, how new the day seems, how right. A cooler arrives, the big round kind that football players dump over their coach's head after a big win. A kind of drink is administered in paper cups—it looks like strawberry preserves. Cold cloths are spread and respread over the foreheads of the fallen ones. True Heart moves from one to the next. The *heyoka* looks like a mean drunk and the *winktes* all sashay tiredly uphill toward the kitchen. The singer who started all this is behind a support beam smoking a cigarette. Nicki's out cold. Her face is white. Chief's on his knees, tending her. Someone moans. The dark-headed woman's crying. Leslie sits in a folding chair with his legs stretched out. He tells a joke. An Indian child pushes a Tonka dumptruck in the dirt along the northern gate. Koo Wan, she's disappeared. I've seen piercings. Now, I've seen the piercings. My stomach burns. Here's the time, my ticket: I could go straight, take on the way of the *canupa*, Sundance, offer flesh—the opportunity lays white-faced cold in front of me. On sorry grass. She's done. As supporter, I must take her place. The rule is the rule. I see Mailman across the ring, he doesn't know yet. A part of me that I know as my core, my true essence, desires nothing in this world but to run like hell, to pack my shit and get out.

Before anything else can happen, this kick-ass thunderstorm, *Wakinyan-tanka*, blows in southwest. Rain falls in fat splats so it's hard to see the tree, and wind rips the roof off the arbor under which lie the stricken dancers. The fireman named Kirk and the lawn and garden salesman join me inside the ring. The blue tarps—our roof—flap unbelievably in the thunder and lightning. The idiot flapping is hard to comprehend, hilarious, a giant blue tongue talking gibberish. Rain stings me. A piece of the eastward sky shines brightly. We set to work with ropes tied to hunks of wood, throwing them from one side of the arbor to the other, then lashing to the support timbers. A dancer ties a rag on his head and puts his shoulder into a rope. Many are collapsed on their backs with their eyes shut, paper cups of spilt medicine leaking on the ground. Yes, the rain has a bite to it. It's cold, that's the way it is out here, a heat furnace one minute, sleet on your head the next. Southwest, the trailing edge of the storm goes silver. By the time we get the roof tied down, the rain stops. Sunlight ruptures the dark clouds, turns the fluting edges coppery-gold and warm light pours over the grounds. Twenty-thousand prayer ties gleam on the silver-fleshed tree. The cross-bar for the one who's dreamed of the eagle dance looks like a crucifix with all these pagan ribbons flapping. Light shimmies in the upper limbs so that it seems very much alive, growing straight down into the earth. The air is clear and clean now, sweet to breathe. The day's a clean slate, that's how it feels.

Nicki moves, just the slightest bit. It's enough. She's alive. I walk uphill to the kitchen shack, drink glass after glass of lemonade until my stomach rolls. The sun comes full out. From under the kitchen tarp I can see my tent. The eight-pointed star glistens. Hopefully to hell it didn't leak on Jill and Lyra's pictures. I smell woodsmoke and summer rain, the rip-thud of thunder and lightning sulfur. I hurt for my wife and my daughter. I hurt for myself. I want us to hold on to each other in a hard rain, breathe the storm-clean air and pray for hope and courage and love. I want wolves to howl. I want to give what is mine to give. I want to forgive and be forgiven. I want the sun to burst through the black cloud and shine on our heads. I want the world to rise up, shake herself off and be new again.

I want to change my life.

12.

Heyokas—the Sacred Clowns—bring laughter to the circle. They marry dead-seriousness to comic truth, and so bring balance. They have powers, the people say, in common with the Thunder Beings, *Wakinyantanka*, and when they come, rain follows. There are very few of them and they mostly stay to themselves, rarely mixing with people. This second, the scar-throated *heyoka* wears *Issiwun*, the sacred buffalo hat. He's all over the *winktes*, goring the bejesus out of them. Near the end of the rest time, True Heart asked Charley to speak. The story was about his *hanbleceya*—his vision quest—which happened at a time when he was nearly blind. After four days and nights on the mountain, a woman came to him, saying, "Stand and behold what you have become." I can tell he's told the story many times, I've heard and seen it myself in a Pentecostal church after the speaking in tongues and snake handling. Another woman talked about how, only recently, she had a crippling disease and could not walk, only love had reentered her life in the form of a man and now, see her, she's *dancing*. Here, at this part in the story, the *heyoka* began to flagellate himself, to really beat the shit out of his calves and thighs with a leather whip made to look like a buffalo tail. "Relatives," he said. "Some of you are laying down. Not paying attention." His right hand sliced air this way and that—Indian hand talk, I've seen white people pick it up, though it looks weird, like a nerd doing the robot dance. "When a relative speaks, sit up and listen. Now get your asses up," he said, fierce-eyed, then stalked around like the dance police. Now he's giving the *winktes* hell, goring their asses with the *Issiwun* hat. "You ain't *heyoka*," he screams, "go both ways."

Nicki sits under the arbor. She's fifty-two, fifty-three, on a blanket in the grass, a colorful shawl wrapped around her neck and shoulders. Mailman's beside her. He's a recovering alcoholic who says lodge is the only thing that keeps him straight. Tall and a little goofy, easily irritated, I picture him carrying a mail sack, somebody's little rat terrier growling under a door, delivering a handful of ads for five dollar pizzas and discount recliners, the lost person notices that say *Have You Seen Me?* beside a photograph doctored to show how the lost are imagined to have aged. For a long time I believed they were mistrustful of me, Nicki and Mailman, that insulation I feel between me and Mormons, even when they quit practicing.

She looks me in the face, still a little loopy, pupils dilated. "You ready to dance?"

Faces turn on me, the moment is white hot.

Words don't come.

"What are you afraid of?" Uncle asked all those years ago, one hand quivering on the fenceline—the volts running him through. I've since read that all impulse is electric, *wakangeli*, pulsing up our spines, whirling through the nuclei of our atoms. When my pee splashed the silver wire, I knew why.

Here's a truth—the horse's mouth: seen from the outside in, ceremony seems brutal, a real hardass way to go. I remember that first vision quest camp, the elaborate funeral ceremony of putting somebody out on a plot of ground, not at all flat, imagining her ever-rolling downhill, no way to sleep or rest or escape the very real sun. Another was near a creek and I pictured him thirsty, hearing the water babble in the afternoon and night and then in the morning when the birds kicked in and he'd dream of his tongue growing to the creek, sipping cool water from a shady hole, then delicately devouring a salamander to squelch the third day fast. But on the inside it's not like that at all. The physicality of it all: blood and flesh and bone. For one thing, you're entirely in now time, in the now, and you don't see yourself as how you might become, but as how you are. Like a girl I used to know on the track team who ordinarily kept herself immaculate, every tooth flossed perfectly, only when running a hundred sets of bleachers one spring afternoon she vomited, just turned her head and puked a nasty load then kept on running, not even wiping her chin; she was in the now, and people in the now couldn't care in the least how you see them.

When Evangeline put me on the mountain, it was raining like a mother, cold rain, big, fat drops. This was Utah; we were at altitude, snow flies all twelve months in Utah. It could snow or sleet any second. The air temperature would drop into low forties that night. Back country hikers died of hypothermia all the live long day. I had no food, no water, no shelter. My blanket was sopping. But all while Evangeline sang my high-pitched death song, I remember thinking *this isn't so bad, not at all, I get to rest now*, and after they left, when I was alone, it really felt good, and then it felt great, being out on that Croydon hillside with the long red bluff falling to the south and east, my daughter down at camp romping with Nicki's granddaughters, though I couldn't know that a microburst had blown a huge cottonwood limb off and knocked big Camille out cold, so the kids all thought she was dead while they put me on the mountain. From the inside, it's not bad, and *now* is a great teacher. I learned in a split second how to lick rain drops from the clefts of tongue-shaped chokecherry leaves, how a bandana dipped in the beaverpool cools the head and thus the whole body, how speaking names out loud brings the spirit of the namesakes near, how you can make peace with awful things like your mother's drowning so they don't seem awful anymore, how you can be okay with yourself and the world and wonder why you've ever worried about anything at all. The inside of now time is Maslov's hierarchy reversed, enlightenment reached by physical needs created and released. Through affliction comes redemption. *Are you ready to dance?* Maybe that's how death is, now time.

"Your dance is over," Mailman says. He's on the ground beside her, loving her. His heart's all there in those words. "True Heart says your dance is over, honey. He hasn't been asked to dance."

It dawns on me that there is a degree of shame in him not supporting his wife. Just a shade. Jill must have felt that with me, as all of us who ever let a loved one down when the moment is at hand. Like how I sometimes feel on the front porch at sundown in the winter, smoking and sipping whiskey in the cold while my family goes on with their lives inside.

That day, in round four, I enter the ring, enter the dance. The *heyoka* takes me around the perimeter, through the lines, shows me how to *azilia* dancers with sweet pungent cedar. "Hold it low," he says. "At their knees." It's sometime in the afternoon and the heat's back, only not so much as before. The dancer's eyes are softened now. Some say thank you, cupping handfuls to their faces. The buffalo blanket is brought out for more piercings, more singings of the *Tunkasila* song, and others, one about a beautiful maiden who danced off a cliff backwards so she could be with her lover who'd been killed in battle: *wicasala wan tewahila k'un, wan weglakin kta hunse*—sweet, incomprehensible words. What I notice with what feels like my heart is the harmonious interweaving of outside and inside. How the supporters under the arbors lift and lower their feet just as the dancers do. How they lift hands and faces to the tree and speak the Lakota words for "thank you for giving us this to do." How the tree shimmers and every point in our circle's circumference is the same distance from a tree where flaps the *winkte*'s penis man over this imitation earth. The sun is at three quarters in the western sky—the light goes gold and there's a stillness as I move through the V's of men and women who thirst. I feel peace, like when what's supposed to happen finally happens. I'm told we carry this peace with us all the time, only—for most of us—there's no clue it's there, so we set out looking high and low for all the things we need to keep on climbing the ladder of this life. We need love and a boatload of courage. We reach and we are reached to. We live, like it or no, in context to our relatives: all beings, all matter. Today, inside the Sundance circle, time backs off a little, lets me glide in and out of the audience and dancers and the *heyoka*'s lead. Without thought, I dance. I lift and lower my feet. My heart beats.

An Indian woman is pierced, eagle feathers inserted through slits in her upper arms. Crowned with sage, her daughter was the first to chop the cottonwood tree. Now the little girl joins her right out on the dance floor and the two dance joyously around the circle—the little girl leaping and laughing like it's Christmas morning, like she's just gotten the greatest gift ever. Many children play around the circle's outside and this is a comfort, I don't know why.

The last one I see pierced is a huge tattooed man with a jet-black pony-tail hanging to his waist. He's six-three, maybe three hundred pounds, the size of the man I saw dragged from the wrecked car. When he's laid out for the cutting, his head and feet hang off either end of the buffalo robe. He's on his back, big breaths heaving in his chest. One of the Lakotas takes off the sage crown, sticks it between the dancer's teeth. From twenty-feet away, I see the incisions made, how the stream of blood is sudden. I'm throwing handfuls of cedar shake in my bucket, moving clockwise from north to south. When the skewers are fitted through the halter loops, the man is led to a position straight southwest. He leans his full weight back. The rope is tight. His skin stretches. He throws his full weight backward, violently, but the flesh won't give. His supporters, one on either side, each grab a huge arm and pull him backward—they lean and shove with all they've got. I'm moving north to south around the perimeter, dizzy. Sandy screams my name just as I'm about to break the eastern gate, one step to spare, one instant from ending the ceremony. From the tree, he makes the sign to stop. The big man walks to the tree, leans into it, touches his nose to the prayer ties. Then he begins to lumber backwards. I'm locked in. He holds both arms out in front of him like a sleep-walker in reverse. Both eyes are wide. His escape from this earth is a leviathan leap of faith and nearly three hundred pounds of bone and muscle and flesh.

The crowd's collective breath is exhaled, as I imagine it was in ancient Greece after the actor playing Oedipus gouged out his eyes, or when

Antigone is joined in suicide by the heartbroken lover. The stage parts, the clowns join the chorus and, their falls complete now, all the tragic heroes are exultant. Catharsis works its way into the very geometry of the Sundance arena, this living theater, this spectacle of energy in motion. The buffalo rug is rolled and taken to the fireman shed. The latex gloves and scalpels and surgical buckets are put away. The big Indian ceases to take flesh offerings near the sapling at the northern gate. Chief Roberto directs the reinactment of the pipe gift ceremony, each *canupa* lifted skyward four times before changing hands. This time I file out with the dancers; neither one of them nor one of the outside, I'm somewhere in-between. Willy Day fans from my bucket as the dancers walk past. He touches my head with *wanbli gleska*. Straight sober, I'm pure as sweetwater. Koo Wan, sun shining through her violet silk, rearranges the wood chunk for True Heart's foot. She nods when our eyes meet—*hoka hey*.

The day ends with a healing round, when each dancer takes the *canupa* and walks the entirety of the perimeter touching the pipe to each onlooker. It takes long, this healing. One woman stops in front of me, stares me straight in the face until I look at the ground. The crazy one with a long braid, who'd worked the chainsaw like a Ginsu knife, he's all energy, on fire, this wild look in his eyes. Roberto leads the dancers through the western gate where the sun shines. "Stick around," Red Holy says when he passes. "The fun's just starting."

Outside, a skull dancer screams at us firemen to move a water bucket. "Get that shit out of my sight," he tells us.

Another winces. "Some days are better than others," he says.

Nicki passes. On her way uphill, away from the dancers, she walks right past. I can't read her, how she feels. We've talked. I've explained how it's time for me to go home, how I miss my wife and daughter, and that my work as her supporter is done here. "Fine, great," Nicki said. "Thank you for what you've done," she told me. Now, another woman, very pretty, collapses near the *inipi* door, asks for a chair. I retrieve a lawn chair from the fire shed and she kicks back, rolls the length of her skirt up on sunburned thighs. She sighs, moans. Truth is, I marvel at the sight of this unshaven hippy woman at sundown in the desert. My heart is filled to aching. She stretches long legs, crosses ankles and shuts her eyes, lets a wrist rest on her forehead, while inside the song lifts and falls to a drumbeat.

13.

Wednesday, July 20, I'm up before sunrise. The Full Buck moon throws my shadow. I see the ant hill now scattered with food scrap in moonlight. My coolers are out under the stars—the ice has held. I place a grape between my teeth and bite, sour-sweet and cold. A gallon of apple juice sloshes as I unscrew the top and take a hard, cold pull that tastes so good my head hurts. I brush teeth, rinse with cold water, take out a clean bandana and wash my face, pull a comb through my hair a few times. I dress barefoot under the moon. The sky is clear and it's very cool and sparks roil from the fire. The catch in my side is gone. My blood pressure's down. Overnight, I've drunk thirty ounces of well-water so my piss is clean and unlabored. I rub lotion on my face, let my headlight shine on Lyra's face, Jill's. I'm going home today, *home*. I won't make it all the way, but I'll get damn close, within striking distance. I'll hear their voices. Who can say the feel of turning home?

I lace on boots, haul out the dripping apple juice and pick my way across the grounds, past a fetid toilet to the kitchen. Florida Boy's on top of things, the coffee's good to go. He flashes a smile, says "morning," so I hear the south in his voice, rain on tin, barbed-wire, persimmons growing on yellow-leafed trees on the afternoon after first frost. Each step closer to the fire has me feeling more thankful than the last, so happy to be here, so happy to be leaving. By the time I'm there I'm downright overflowing with generosity, and offer the first man I see the whole goddamn jugful of apple juice.

Only it's Hawk, the lame Sundancer, sitting in the lawn chair that I unfolded yesterday, talking about how he's just discovered he's Eskimo. "Sure thing," he says, "if you really want me to have it." The stick he walks on lays at his feet. You never forget that first full day without water, how you curse the sky for not pissing in your face.

"I'm sorry."

"No problem," Hawk says, slips back into his story.

He's having *heyoka* dreams. When this is all over, he's driving his car up to Alaska to meet Eskimos. Operation Desert Storm won't leave him alone. I'm pretty sure he's crazy, mentally ill, and I'm pretty sure a good many of the people I've met here are the same. *Much madness is divinest sense.* Should anybody on the outside see me now, lock-up city. I carry the apple juice to the fire shed, hide it under a blanket. Then I roll a cigarette, sit on the ground and smoke. What gives me the right to be here? When a fire's burning, why do I feel inside like it's mine? Who owns fire? And these ceremonies—how is it that I keep falling through the seams into their insides?

Many faces, I see now, reflect firelight. Robert, Sundance headman, his face materializes, Sandy, Willy Day. True Heart is here, moving through the dark, energy in motion. The Kiowa boy—Hawk's nephew—works the fire. The faintest skiff of pink sky bleeds through the east, light soon.

Dancers congregate outside the lodge doors. Hernando leads the men in and asks for seven stones. I grab a pitchfork, slide it under a *tunka* half the size of a bowling ball, a nice rock, glowing. This job, carrying the stones, it used to awe me to watch the firemen lift a rock out of the fire, blow ash off with a stiff breath, then slide it on the pitchfork tongs through the *inipi* door onto the medicine wheel. And when you're inside looking out, the fire's dancing against the sky and cool air and birdsong and green grass blows in on you. A *womb*, like being dead and alive, that's how it is looking out the *inipi* door. Fireman's in-between—he can shut the door, he can open the door. I carry a white-hot stone, a *tunka*, the oldest thing I know.

Sun rises on the buffalo skulls.

They've been laid out all around the fire, huge horned heads with hollow eye sockets and scraps of dried meat and sinew. Seven of them circle the fire, facing outward. I've heard how men drag them, how they pierce themselves front and back and tie buffalo skulls to the ropes and halters. How they run round the Sundance grounds with the *heyokas* and clowns and the headman keeps on tying on buffalo skulls until the skewers break free. Sometimes, I've been told, a man's flesh can bear the weight of all seven buffalo skulls, and then the children are called out from under the arbors and they gleefully climb onto the skulls and ride the strange merry-go round until the buffalo dancer's stubborn flesh gives.

"*Here.*" The one who'll skull dance today is on hands and knees just inside the *inipi* door. He's thirsty. He's not at all happy. He makes a cross in the dirt with one finger, then pounds it with a palm. "Right goddamn *here*," he screams.

The scars on his back are the size of half-dollars.

"*Here,*" he screams when I bring the second stone, lightning hot, so tines of his deer antlers scorch when he scoops up the rock and forks it into the pit. He pounds the earth with a fist.

In the fierce mirror our minds make, I reflect the buffalo dancer's fury straight back on him. With my whole soul, I turn his fury back. I take the energy, turn it back.

While lifting the next rock, his back goes out. I hear it crack, an odd pop like when the cottonwood started to fall. He's hauled out under the arbor where a clown-faced *winkte* lights sage and works his body for the remainder of the round. If I feel remorse, it's mixed with awe. *Wakangeli* lept through me, down the man's spine to the base of his back.

For the second round of the sweat-in, the buffalo dancer sits in the folding chair beside the firepit, using a cedar branch to brush ash off the stones I carry. Our eyes have met. We both know the wrong we've done, and with this knowledge comes a peace, the sort shared by those who've fought until their blood is free of anger.

Again the deep-voiced drum sounds from the dance circle's southern side, and the old song begins again as the sun rises and the dancers are led around the perimeter to the eastern gate where they look up and behold the tree now risen bright and terrible. Faces are solemn now—there's none of yesterday's lightness. *Heyoka* has disappeared, he won't return to this ceremony. Ropes flutter from the tree's crossbar. "We'll make a man fly like a bird up there," he'd said, grinning that wicked grin, same shape as the scar where his neck's been slit.

The dancers enter the ring in sober formation, V-ing the four directions. They sing *Tunkasila*, holding hands upward to the tree, saying *pilamaya yelo hey*.

A strange place, this earth.

I track down Sandy, thank him for letting me be a fireman. He's under the kitchen tent pulling on a hooded sweat shirt, joking how he gets cold when he's away from the fire too long.

We shake. "Why you leaving?"

"I miss my family."

"Me too."

And that's that. Like everyone else I'll talk to, he knows that people aren't supposed to come and go, especially ones who've been in cere-mony—it fucks up the energy, the dynamic, the balance. Koo Wan would feel the difference straight away. I *need* to hold my daughter in my arms. And I *need* to before True Heart looks me in the eye, sees what lies in the depth of my heart, beckons with his old withered hand and whispers the words, then looks me in the face and waits.

Straight away the buffalo robe is hauled out and the piercings start. I find Mailman standing under the arbor with the Utah group. He smiles, shakes my hand. "You know," he tells me. "You could always walk up to Chief. Tell him you've had the dancing dream. There's no reason you can't dance if you want to."

Mailman looks at me, smiles that goofy smile that's got a touch of smirk in it. He's testing me, I'm sure of that.

Out on the floor, Hernando slices the chest of a man laid down on the buffalo robe. "It's like one long surgery," I say.

"Yeah," he says, grins. "And today the eagle dancer flies." He points up to the crude cross where a tremendous skein of red cloth flaps.

He's wearing the black ball cap I've given him because he forgot to bring hats out into the desert. A mailman who forgets his hat. Mailman, standing there watching the mutilations in my black hat.

Today, the man named Kirk is to be pierced, as is Red Holy. Behind us this second, Kirk's blonde wife, his daughter and son, huddle together, look terror-stricken. When Hernando laces the skewers through the man's chest, the wife looks as if she'll die. Her daughter's crying. How could anybody put their family through this? How can you make your people watch you be crucified? I couldn't do it to Jill, not Lyra. This green bottle glass grates my thigh. One day I'll watch this blonde wife dance to a tree, the terrified daughter will pierce. What do I know on this earth?

I fight the urge to say goodbyes and break camp quickly. The first round ends as I'm loading and people come streaming uphill for breakfast. Just as I finish, Willy Day says my name and we meet between our camps. He's tall, full Lakota and has himself, this year, finished a fourth year of dancing at the Horse Sanctuary in South Dakota. He's dressed as the dancers in a long red skirt, an eagle feather tied into long black hair. Last night I met his son who has this unbelievably distinct memory for the details of certain motion pictures. Yesterday, he motioned me onto the dance floor many times; I stood beside him as he fanned cedar smoke from my bucket to strengthen the dancers, to help them out. I like this man—he's funny, a stone mason.

"Leaving?" he says in a low voice.

I say, "Yeah. The woman I'm supporting, Nicki, she's out of the dance now."

We shake hands. He nods, looks into my eyes for a second. And the shame hits me and the fear all at once. He knows—and it's okay. In his eyes it registers, and I believe he's felt the same way I do now, just wanting to go home.

"Thanks for bringing me in," I say.

He says, "Sure."

"Those buffalo skulls. I'd like to see that dance."

Willy Day smiles, "Stick around and you will." He turns and walks off toward the kitchen where I smell eggs and bacon and coffee. I shake out a handful of tobacco and let it fall on the bent grass and pine needles where my tent has been. Then I get in the Pathfinder, shut the door and start the engine. The red letters on the digital clock say ten o'clock—straight up. When I drive off I have this sensation of being chased, of many beings chasing me, running me down, willing me to stay. They are furious, the spirits. As I leave ceremony, a hundred, a thousand beings, pissed beyond belief, they scream behind me. The souls of all the dead rage behind my back. They feel like fire. They *are* fire. Here's as close as I get, and still leave. Wolf, spirit, the red road—the whole goddamn nine yards—*real*. Driving way too fast, rolling four windows up at once, I'm sure of it. Real. Ahead of me is the Cougar ranch sign, only I'm seeing the reverse side for the first time. A dust cloud rises behind me.

Live in Beauty, the sign says. Live in beauty?

14.

Between Gallup and Shiprock I come across a broken down family—Navajo, the father fiddling under the hood with battery cables. The car's a junker. I pass, then hang a U-turn, pull in just ahead of them. Inside, a little boy and girl in the sweltering back seat, the mother in a cotton skirt up front. The sky is pale blue—all morning I've been passing east-facing hogans, their turquoise front doors facing the rising sun. I fish the four remaining lemonades from fresh ice in the cooler, walk back and give them to the broken down family. How many times have I been this way with Mama? Once at the Razorback Twin Drive-In outside of Jacksonville, Arkansas— Dr. Zhivago belting out "Laura's Theme" on one screen and some R-rated booby movie on the other. Me on the playground in-between, on an errand to bring Mama a cold drink. It was August in Arkansas, the heat was hell on wheels, and we'd come to the drive-in seeking sanctuary. The horn on our Pontiac had somehow got stuck on. Mama believed it would just go away. People were getting pissed. I remember how the playground swing squeaked a little as I swung back and forth, bare breasted girls flouncing on the eastern screen while these sad-faced Russians inhabited a fake ice palace in the west, and the blare of our broken down car.

"No thank you," the mother says, but she takes the lemonades, as does the man under the hood. The cans pop open, they drink like people dying of thirst in the desert.

"Give me a jump?" he says.

I turn my Pathfinder around, connect up to him and try to jump him off for thirty minutes or so. Poor people are experts at jumping cars off, I've done it with every make, learned the trick of parking a stick shift on a hill for a drift start. I've jumped off every piece of shit you can dream of, and even owned a sea-green Volvo you could start with a screw driver. And me and this Indian daddy, we try hard. I let it run, pump the accelerator, undo the positive cable and carve off corroded lead until the connection shines. But this car won't start—she's dead. He disconnects the battery and puts it on an old shirt inside the Pathfinder's hatch. I leave him at the first garage we see in Shiprock, and feel better about myself. I slide in a jazz CD I've brought, Wynton Marsalis, something about "our fathers." Maybe if I help everybody I ever see from here on out, if I go out of my way for the rest of my life to help anybody who needs a hand, I can satisfy what chased me from the Sundance—I can make whatever *that* was lie down and be quiet. If I help enough, it'll be okay.

From Shiprock I drive west across the Navajo Nation—the reservation highway through Teec Nos Pos, Red Mesa, Mexican Water and Dennehotso. I pass the black spot where I witnessed the giant Indian being cut out of a flipped car five days ago, and remember how one wheel was still spinning when I got there. The San Juan is muddy when I cross the bridge into Utah. Reservation gas at White Mesa is cheapest, so I fill up there, wait in line for the toilet, then chew a handful of grapes and head north. There's a quiet spot people talk about after ceremony, where your mind is quiet and at ease and you nod your head and say, yeah, it's okay. That's the way I'm feeling all across that great plateau that falls into Moab where the Colorado River turns desert into oasis, and the light shines off red rock spires, domes and cliffs in ways that nothing made by hands can rival. By the time I hit Moab I'm feeling peaceful as Jesus, at ease with myself. Spirit is long-gone behind me, surely. The opening that tree created is as good as closed for me now. It's five in the afternoon, going on six—I've been working since long before light. Don't I deserve to rest, why push too hard?

City Market Grocery is on the right when you're driving north; I park under a shade tree, go into the cool insides and push a cart slowly between aisles, lingering over loose leaf lettuce and red onions, good salsa, cans of vegetarian chili and cheddars on the cheese aisle, what I'll need for a nacho salad. This is outdoor country—everybody looks rough. On my skin, I smell this morning's smudge, a whiff of cedar from the dance. The world is a good world, *metakuye oyasin.*

For the first time in my life, I choose self-check out. I start scanning items and have a hell of a time with the produce buttons, then can't get the machine to take a fifty. A brown-eyed woman helps me out, she takes my money and gives me change. "Please take your receipt and remove your bag," an airless voice says, so that the machine-cooled air, and fluorescent soft light, and display magazines, and bloodless meats under too clean glass are revealed as frauds outright. Going to ceremony's one thing, coming back from that world's another. Traced on me—earth, air, fire and water, tree, ant people, rattlesnake brother, magpie jabber and the ruckus eagle wings make when beating. The *Tunkasila* song's in my heart, as is the howling of wolves, the sound tearing flesh makes.

Outside, I call home collect, dial my own phone number and say my name into the receiver. What I need most in this world is exactly what I get. "You're *okay,*" Jill says when she answers, then, "It's Daddy, Lyra. Daddy's on the phone," so that I can tell she means it, that there's love in her heart for me still and she's missed me and my home is still my home. Lyra says, "Daddy? I *missed* you. I made a surprise for you."

Jill says, "We've missed you so much."

Her voice can be hard: once in a blizzard and again in a hurricane, I called her a little happy just to say I love you. And both times she hung up. The first time, from a phone outside in the snow, she said, "I'm busy." The second time, with the hard wind in my face, she hung up and I stood there like an idiot saying *hello* into the dead line. Straight sober, I'd wept. But now she's sweet, and I can hear the wine on her tongue.

"So you'll be home tonight?"

It's going on six, happy hour now, the cool grass going shady green in our backyard. This is Lyra's favorite time of day for play, mine too. "Make me fly again, Daddy," she'll say. "Watch me climb the tree. Introducing Lyra, the famous trapeze girl." I tell my wife where I'm calling from, that I'm in Moab now, that I've been up since four. It's been more than I imagined. I'll camp the river and be home inside of noon tomorrow. I say *I love you*.

"We *love* you," she says. "Be careful."

"I will."

"Good," Jill says.

Today, I choose to believe in love.

The sun's headed west, it's not in my eyes at all. Redrock shines from here to the Manti-La Sal. Castle Valley's up there. I'm as pure as river water. My mind's as clear this second as it will ever be, I know that, and I'm choosing to believe in *love*.

I cruise through a stop light, hit the liquor store for vodka, then drive on out to the edge of town and take 128 north along the Colorado River. A sign explains how the name Moab is after the incestuous child born of Job and his daughters. After Sodom and Gomorrah, they'd wandered the wilderness for a long time, and never seen anyone. So the daughters got antsy for love and marriage and babies, and schemed to take their father to a cave where they'd make him drunk with wine and have their way. Drunk with love, their carnal wish came true. The boy child's name was Moab, for whom this town is named.

Matrimony Springs is on the right about a mile up, sweet spring water gushing out a huge rock on the side of the road; drink the water, you're married to it. This stretch of river is honestly breathtaking—we came here at Christmastime, me, Jill and Lyra, stayed in Castle Valley up river, a salt dome that sixty million years ago rose up in a tremendous bubble, then fell leaving the most beautiful valley you could imagine. The highway skirts the blue, clean river where rafters sail by from the put-in at Hittle Bottom, a daily run with campsites right on the water. We stayed here before Lyra was born, me and Jill. It was spring break, our first year in Utah, and we'd camped the night before in the mud near Boulder Mountain. I'd got us stuck in a snow drift on top of Devil's Backbone. A farmer from the valley'd had to haul us out. We drove the highway to Green River and somehow got pulled down into Moab and the river—I don't know what we were looking for. Our gear was a mess. We burned a woodfire and bathed naked in the river, then argued long and hard about everything and nothing in particular, we did our damndest to hurt each other with words. Part of love is learning where the skin is thinnest, the mark we aim for when anger comes. After the fight, I'd guzzled wine and slept outside the tent, and even out there, Jill'd come out in the night. "Quit snoring," she'd said.

Today, I find the perfect site, a table and flat ground for the tent, then a slight grade down to the river where there's a sandy beach and good eddy for bathing. It's very hot and I make fast work of setting camp, pitch the tent flyless and unroll my bag, unwrap the photographs of my wife and daughter. A raven flaps overhead and I can hear a troop of camp kids eating supper over at the group site. I set the stove for cooking, lay the water can on its side, haul out my cooler and a camp chair, make my way to the river where I wade in until the water's over my head, a clean, cold shock that must be the most ancient of joys. Not far upstream a ripple swishes and the sun is still five handwidths above the red sandstone cliffs to the west. Underwater, I massage the grit from my scalp, a little current in the eddy spinning me toward a sand island where a child's footprints walk away from an elaborate sand castle. The afternoon is perfect. I'm not lonely, not at all. The dancers are through their second day now, sweating out, thirsty and hungry—I'm so glad to be away from there, so glad I went. In my head, the song repeats over and over, *Tunkasila, pilamaya yelo hey*. Hands are raised to the tree.

The beach sand is warm. I unfold the camp chair, open the cooler, ice my camp mug and make a stiff vodka tonic. The lime I slice is pungent—I can smell it mixing with the vodka and fizzing tonic water. I sit with the sun in my face and roll a cigarette, light it and inhale. Part of me prays for the dancers and another part prays for myself. The raven chases a sparrow over the river then glides into a long drawn out fall before lighting on a boulder on the river's other side. The drink is good. Very, very good. Quinine from the tonic blends with the citrus and there's the vodka's bite. I smoke the tobacco from ceremony, drink the ice-blue vodka and feel it work on me straight away. "Hello, brother raven," I say out loud, and the son-of-a-bitch *caw-caw-caws.* That's how it is on the river this afternoon—my life is as it should be, that's what I'm believing. Every now and then I wade into the river, let myself sink under water. Each time the water is heavenly and I think, *whoa,* be careful. Be careful. And each time I get out the sand is warm on my feet and the tonic fizzes over fresh ice and the lime is sweet and sour and I drink deep and feel very good about being alive.

A family shares the site above me, I see them addling down the wooded trail to my beach, a father, two children. I fold the chair, haul my cooler up to camp, then come back down with a tub for dishwashing water. The children are tanned, good looking, they splash through the water to the sand island, go to work on the castle. The mother's nowhere to be seen.

"Howdy," the man says. "I get all my water from that spring up the road."

I say, "This is for washing. It's good, isn't it."

"Yeah," he says.

I tell him to take care, walk uphill and make my dinner, a nacho salad laced with real sour cream and salsa, heavy shakes of tabasco, washed down with big gulps of vodka tonic. The sun sets and I build a driftwood fire. The family in the site above me eats dinner, their forks tink-tinking against metal plates. I can hear them talking, the woman's voice now. For some reason, I take my vision quest bundle out of the Pathfinder, unwrap it and look at each object by firelight. They'd put me on the mountain in a hard rain and wind. We're talking Croydon, Utah—not so far from the Uintas—where snow falls in every month. It was cold. Evangeline, the Mandan woman, sang out the high, eerie eagle voice behind my back as I faced West in my grave plot.

I'd stashed a stone in my boot from Mama's grave, one I'd dug up myself while laying the blocks my people have ever lain around each other—something to do, good work taking care of your dead, keeping the tomb. And this stone I'd brought was unusual. It was deep-hued purple, a color Mama loved, and these colorful ridges made a perfect three-quarter circle. That's why I saved the stone to begin with, and why I brought it with me up on the mountain, I don't know, except that maybe I knew that I had some work to do, making peace with her drowning, with not being able to say goodbye. Many times I'd felt her presence. Maybe she would come. Maybe her spirit would seal our farewell.

When they left me on the mountain, the rain stopped and the sun came out and the world got so bright it was hard to stand. Fierce hummingbirds dive-bombed the cloth strips I'd ripped and tied to the chokecherry saplings on each of my four corners. They hovered in front of my face. One stuck its pink tongue into the tobacco bundle I was to keep in my right hand until spirit took it away, that's how I'd know it was time, when spirit took the prayer bundle from my hand. When it got dark, I covered with the star blanket. I stood for a long time under full-blown Milky Way. I talked to myself, said the names of people I've loved. Then I got sleepy and lay down with the tobacco bundle tied into the palm of my right hand. The ground was uneven so I kept sliding downhill, falling into the protective tobacco lines Evangeline had sprinkled to make the boundaries of my grave. When I shut my eyes a dream came, I can't remember it, though it didn't seem important at the time—people were in this dream, men and women. And when I woke the tobacco tie had been taken from my hand; the prayer bundle was gone. Evangeline said that this was when you know your vision has come: the world cracks open and truth shines through.

The light came and a strange thing happened. My feet were cold so I laced on the boots I'd used to hike up the mountain. And the stone— Mama's stone—hurt my foot so I took it out. There it was in my hand, maybe four inches across, a purple stone that made three-quarters of a perfect circle. Embedded in the ground was a stone of the same color, an exact match. When I sat Mama's stone on top of the other, it fit in exactly. I mean, the goddamn thing actually clicked into place so that what I saw was a perfect purple circle, complete now. I've never told anyone this, my vision. And I don't know what it means, except that something ended there on the mountain in Croydon, Utah. And something began.

Now, the white liquor whizzing through my blood and the stars out shining, I feed each of the objects I've saved from my *hanbleceya* into the driftwood fire. Weeping, I don't know why, I burn it all and the fire is bright when the cloth catches. I hear Evangeline singing my death song and know that anyone who has ever loved me would love this.

Uphill, the couple fights. They've put their kids to bed and are going at each other, screaming awful things. This instant the wolf's voice comes howling out of my mouth and I'm on hands and knees in the dirt by the dancing fire, howling up at the full Buck Moon with all my heart, all my soul, every cell in my body howling. My howl is *wakan*, it echoes off the cliffsides so I hear myself calling out to myself. For a long time, I howl.

When I wake up the fire's gone, and I'm laid out in the dirt, cold, shivering. I crawl into the tent, zip into my sleeping bag and sleep hard. It's almost nine by the time I get up. The family uphill is long gone. I wonder what they'll say, if this will be a story they carry with them through their lives, how a man at the campsite next to them wolf-howled, and when they checked on him he was passed out in the dirt by a dying fire. Were they afraid? Had they packed in the dark and driven themselves to a hotel in town? Am I bad medicine?

I'm packed in fifteen minutes. Before leaving, before driving home to my wife and daughter, I wash my face in cold river water. *Omakiya yo,* I say, and dunk into the chill.

Help me.

Here ends the first part of White Indians, the return of Pahana, the lost white brother prophesied by the Hopi and other tribes. The second part tells of the last days and end of the fourth world.

About the Author

A first generation college student, Michael Gills earned his B.A. from the University of Arkansas. He was Randall Jarrell Fellow at the M.F.A. Program at the University of North Carolina-Greensboro, and received his Ph.D. in fiction writing from the University of Utah. His first collection of short  fiction, *Why I Lie*, was published by University of Nevada Press in 2002. It won a Utah Book Prize and was chosen as a top literary debut by *The Southern Review*. Raw Dog Screaming Press released a novel, *Go Love*, in 2011. A second story collection, *The Death of Bonnie and Clyde*, was published by Texas Review Press in 2012; the title story won *Southern Humanities Review*'s Hoepfner Prize for the best story published in 2010. Currently Gills is Associate Professor/Lecturer of Writing for the Honors College at the University of Utah.

www.ingramcontent.com/pod-product-compliance
Lightning Source LLC
Chambersburg PA
CBHW050902180626
46814CB00007B/2855